LA FIESTA DE LOS TASTOANES

OLGA NÁJERA-RAMÍREZ

La Fiesta de
los Tastoanes

CRITICAL ENCOUNTERS IN
MEXICAN FESTIVAL PERFORMANCE

✧ ✧ ✧

University of New Mexico Press Albuquerque

Dedico este libro con todo cariño y respeto para
mi querido profesor, Don Américo Paredes, quien ha sabido
ser un gran maestro en todo el sentido de la palabra.

Library of Congress Cataloging-in-Publication
Nájera-Ramírez, Olga.
La fiesta de los tastoanes : critical encounters in
Mexican festival performance / Olga Nájera-Ramírez.—1st ed.

p.   cm.

ISBN: 0-8263-1795-2 / ISBN: 0-8263-1998-X (pbk.)

Includes bibliographical references and index.
1. Indians of Mexico—Mexico—Jocotán—Rites and ceremonies.
2. Indians of Mexico—Mexico—Jocotán—Religion.
3. Festivals—Mexico—Jocotán.
4. Cargo cults—Mexico—Jocotán.
5. Jocotán (Mexico)—History.
6. Jocotán (Mexico)—Social life and customs.
I. Title   F1219.1.J63N35   1997
394.26972'35 — dc21   97-4615
CIP

Contents

Maps & Figure

Acknowledgments

I am deeply indebted to the many people who contributed to this project since its inception over fifteen years ago. In Mexico, I thank the people of Jocotán for allowing me to study their festival and for offering me valuable insights and perspective on the significance of the festival. I am especially grateful to my very special friends in Guadalajara — Hector Anaya, Martin Muñoz Macias, Luis Mario Fuentes, Luz Maria Alfonso, Lupe and Armando Cornejo, and Lupita Bayardo — for opening up their homes and hearts to me during my many visits and for assisting me in countless ways. I also thank Professors Guillermo de la Peña and Ramón Mata Torres for their invaluable visits in the field.

In the United States, I worked on the book at several universities. I have been fortunate in having the constant support, encouragement, and counsel of several colleagues and friends whom I first met at the University of Texas at Austin. Foremost among these are Beverly J. Stoeltje, José Limón, Richard Flores, Frances Terry, James Brow, Ramón Saldívar, and, of course, Américo Paredes. At the University of California at Berkeley, I had the opportunity of working with Stanley Brandes during my tenure as a Chancellor's Ethnic Minority Postdoctoral Fellow. At UC Santa Cruz, I thank my colleagues Hayden White, David Schneider, and Susan Harding for providing comments on earlier incarnations of the manuscript. I am especially grateful to Diane Gifford-Gonzalez, Shelly Errington, Carolyn Martin-Shaw, and Anna Tsing for inviting me to participate in their writing group. It is through them that I met Kathy Chetkovich, whose assistance proved invaluable in revising the manuscript.

Most of all, I thank my family for keeping the faith. My mother deserves special recognition for enabling me to indulge in the writing process by taking care of my home and my family. I thank my husband Ronaldo and our daughter Elisa for their love and patience; my sisters, Elena and Alicia, for their open hearts and minds; and my brothers Roberto, Martin, and John, and my nieces, Jasmine, Monica, Breena, and Shelly for reminding me of the larger audience for whom I write.

LA FIESTA DE LOS TASTOANES

First Encounters

↓

The shrill sounds of the *chirimía* (double-reed flute) announced that the fiesta was in full swing—somewhere. Filled with anticipation, I jumped off the bus that had brought me from Guadalajara to Jocotán and I followed the music until I came upon a rather large crowd gathered in the church atrium. Elbowing my way through the crowd, I came face-to-face with a wild group of people wearing multicolored masks with long stringy hair, swinging long machetes at each other and toward the onlookers. Almost five hundred years after the Spanish conquest, the Tastoanes were vividly reenacting the heroic struggle of their indigenous ancestors to maintain control over their territory, their resources, their local customs, and, ultimately, themselves. Playfully, they tapped bystanders with their swords and howled with delight as children ran screaming in fear. The masks and swords scared me, too. Even though I knew they were "just playing," I kept my distance.

Stepping back, I noticed that the Tastoanes wore tennis shoes. It seemed absurd to juxtapose traditional attire, such as the animal-like masks, with something so mundane and modern as the tennis shoes in this particular way. Even more distracting was the audience: people came and went as they pleased, continuing with their everyday chores while this ancient fiesta unfolded before their eyes. I felt confused. Exactly what was the point of this celebration? Was this festival an active expression of resistance to the conquest? Or was I witnessing the feeble remains of an ancient rite? Was this, in fact, a painful reminder of the Spanish conquest of the native population? The search for answers to these questions would bring me back to this Jocotán festival time and again over the next ten years.

The Festival

La Fiesta de los Tastoanes dramatically reenacts the political and religious conflicts that arose during the Spanish conquest. When Spain invaded Mexico with the goal of imposing Spanish rule on the native populations in the name of Christianity, disputes broke out between the two groups concerning land ownership, acceptable forms of religious practice, and control of resources. Now, over the course of the three-day La Fiesta de los Tastoanes, these conflicts are manifested publicly in a series of *jugadas*, or mock battles, between Santiago (or St. James, the patron saint of Spain) and the Tastoanes. (The word *tastoanes* derives from the Nahuatl word *tlatoani*, meaning spokespersons, or leaders. During the conquest, it was the tlatoani of this region who led the natives in battles against the Spanish invaders.)

As a religious festival featuring Santiago and dealing with the theme of conquest in the name of Christianity, La Fiesta de los Tastoanes has been classified as a variant of the festival of the *moros y cristianos* (Moors and Christians), which is still celebrated throughout Spain and its former colonies around the world (Kurath 1949b and Warman 1972). Nonetheless, La Fiesta de los Tastoanes features specific characters and costumes, as well as a unique name, that make it recognizable by both scholars and locals as an entity in its own right with multiple variations of its own.

In years past, variations of the Tastoanes festival could be found in many communities surrounding the city of Guadalajara, which is in the state of Jalisco, and even extending into the bordering states of Michoacán and Zacatecas (Map 1). Today, however, only a few communities continue to celebrate this festival. Furthermore, the specific ways and reasons for which it is celebrated in Jocotán remain unique. Most, but not all, Tastoanes festivals occur on or around July 25, Santiago's official saint's day. Tastoanes festivals celebrated on other dates typically pay homage to other saints or virgins. But not in Jocotán. Although Jocoteños specifically honor Santiago, they celebrate La Fiesta de los Tastoanes on September 8, 9, and 10. Here, locals regard Santiago as their special protector, in effect claiming him as their patron saint.[1] It is also worth noting that La Fiesta de los Tastoanes is a community-based festival; that is, it is produced by and for the people of Jocotán and is not controlled by the church or any state agency.

One of my driving concerns has been to establish why the festival persists in Jocotán and to understand its relevance for present-day Jocoteños. For instance, how is it that Santiago, introduced as leader of the Spaniards, has become a special protector of the Jocoteños? How does this festival shape

Map 1

the social memory of the Spanish conquest in Jocotán? How do Jocoteños regard the intersection of two distinct racial, political, religious, and cultural systems? And where do Jocoteños position themselves within this intersection? Are they Spanish or are they Indian, Catholic or pagan, winners or losers? Can they be both?

A comprehensive study of La Fiesta de los Tastoanes offers answers to these critical questions. La Fiesta de los Tastoanes clearly falls within the category of public display events or, in Singer's terms, "cultural performances" (1972). Defined as temporally and spatially bounded, such scheduled public events demand intense participation and attention.[2] Bauman, in his review of performance literature, characterizes cultural performances as metacultural presentations "in which members of society put their culture on display for themselves and others in performance" (Bauman 1986, 133). Hence, cultural performances, such as festivals, contain important information about a community. Bauman explains:

> they are cultural forms about culture, social forms about society, in which the central meanings and values of a group are embodied, acted out and laid open to examination and interpretation in symbolic form, both by members of that group and by the ethnographer. (Bauman 1986, 133)

Since cultural performances involve intense participation in the display, reflection, and interpretation of "the central meanings and values of a group," cultural performances also constitute important sites for analyzing the cultural process. That is, festivals may be approached as important sites in which the ideas and values of the group are not merely displayed but, more importantly, transmitted, produced, and reproduced. Such a view of cultural performance resonates with the findings of social historians, such as Peter Burke, E.P. Thompson, Natalie Z. Davis, George Rudé, and James Scott, who understand popular expressive behavior as an important domain for the articulation of ideology. Consistent with these understandings, Raymond Williams insists that we examine cultural practice in relation to larger domains of power, such as the state. This, in turn, raises questions about the process by which meanings and values become "central" to a group. Gramsci's notion of hegemony, as explicated by Raymond Williams, focuses on the process by which consensus is achieved, challenged, or negotiated over time. Consequently, the notion of hegemony adds significantly to an analysis of cultural performance, in this instance, La Fiesta de los Tastoanes.

The Hegemonic Process

Because Williams's concept of hegemony serves as the underlying theoretical framework within which I understand the festival, I will elaborate on it here. Essentially, Williams describes hegemony as the complex process through which a dominant group imposes its values, beliefs, and interests upon the rest of society by creating, appropriating, or otherwise controlling the various cultural institutions through which the members of a society are socialized. In this way, the hegemonic order pervades society as the natural — if not necessarily correct — order of the world. Nonetheless, according to Williams, the hegemonic process is never complete, for it is constantly being contested and negotiated by the dominated groups. Moreover, in the struggle for hegemony, appropriation occurs by both the dominant and the dominated groups. Williams explains:

> A lived hegemony is always a process. It is not, except analytically, a system or a structure. It is a realized complex of experiences, relationships and activities, with specific and changing pressures and limits. In practice, that is, hegemony can never be singular. Its internal structures are highly complex, as can readily be seen in any concrete anal-

ysis. Moreover (and this is crucial, reminding us of the necessary thrust of the concept), it does not just passively exist as a form of dominance. It has continually to be renewed, recreated, defended, and modified. It is also continually resisted, limited, altered, challenged by pressures not at all its own. We have then to add to the concept of hegemony the concepts of counter hegemony and alternative hegemony, which are real and persistent elements of practice. (1977, 112)

Alternative hegemony refers to alternative ways of living within the established order without directly attempting to challenge the dominant order. Oppositional or counterhegemony rejects the established hegemonic order and attempts to replace it. Particularly relevant to our discussion is Williams's notion of residual culture, which provides a source for the development of either alternative or oppositional hegemony.[3]

The residual, by definition, has been effectively formed in the past but it is still active in the cultural process, not only and often not at all as an element of the past, but as an effective element of the present. Thus certain experiences, meanings, and values which cannot be expressed or substantially verified in terms of the dominant culture, are nevertheless lived and practiced on the basis of the residue — cultural as well as social — of some previous social and cultural institution or formation. (1977, 122)

In a colonial situation, indigenous practices exist as elements of a previous social and cultural formation. By definition, indigenous culture becomes "residual" and therefore constitutes a potential threat to the dominant hegemony. The struggle to maintain indigenous cultural practices in colonial and postcolonial Jocotán therefore assumes political significance. Williams's concept of hegemony thus provides a language and framework within which to discuss the complex history and nature of La Fiesta de los Tastoanes as an important social process relating to issues of power, identity, historical change, and experience.

Hybridization[4]

Drawing on the theories noted above, I argue that La Fiesta de los Tastoanes constitutes a hybrid form which emerged during the Spanish conquest and which exhibits both indigenous and Spanish features. Prior to the

conquest, indigenous festivals tended to be large, communal affairs, bridg-
ing the secular and the religious, the individual and the communal, the past
and the present. Festivals served as powerful expressions of indigenous
religious beliefs, and they also functioned as local forms of historical documentation. During the conquest, the Spaniards discovered that they could
make use of indigenous forms, such as festivals, to communicate new religious and political ideals, and that doing so was more effective than simply
destroying or erasing indigenous elements. Thus, in their efforts to colo-
nize Mexico (and other parts of the New World) the Spaniards superimposed their own *moros y cristianos* dance–drama on existing indigenous celebrations to convey their religious and political superiority and thus convert
their subject populations.

Briefly, the *moros y cristianos* dance–drama celebrates the Spanish Christians' defeat of the Moorish people who had occupied the Iberian Peninsula for almost seven centuries. As a dualist model, the Moors and Christians dance–drama reinforces a simplistic opposition in which the Spanish
Christians represent all that is good, while the "other" assumes those qualities which the Spaniards perceive as evil or otherwise undesirable. Those
who resist conversion become the evil "other"; the model allows for nothing in between.[5]

The native response to this dance–drama, and to the missionizing forces
it represents, was to resist by actively retaining as many indigenous practices as possible. As a result, La Fiesta de los Tastoanes emerged as a hybrid
form, encompassing multiple meanings and contradictions. Hybridization
allows for the simultaneous acceptance of polar extremes in a given continuum or concept, making possible multifarious readings of symbols. Hence,
Santiago is both Spanish conqueror and native healer; the Tastoanes are
both uncivilized animals and brave resisters of subjugation. La Fiesta de los
Tastoanes is both indigenous and Christian, allowing Jocoteños to accept
the framework of Christianization and conquest, yet infuse this framework
with subversive elements.

Hybridization may also stimulate the development of something new.
Thus, with respect to identity, Jocoteños are neither exclusively indigenous
nor exclusively Spanish: rather, as *mestizos*, they occupy an alternative, hybrid position.[6] From this vantage point, Jocoteños may draw upon two
cultural systems to create new symbols or to transform meanings of pre-
existing symbols. Through La Fiesta de los Tastoanes, Jocoteños provide
an alternative to the "all-or-nothing, either/or framework" of the *moros y
cristianos* dance–drama. Festival participants highlight hybridization as a
resolution or alternative to the problems and contradictions of operating

within a polarized framework. By creating a space between two systems, the festival provides an arena for presenting an alternative to those meanings and practices advanced or promoted by the dominant culture through institutional channels such as the church, the media, and the educational system. As such, La Fiesta de los Tastoanes both allows for resistance to and accommodation of the dominant social order and plays an important role in the ongoing struggle over hegemony.

I hope to show that for Jocotán, La Fiesta de los Tastoanes is the means through which community members address various fundamental and ideological concerns, including: (1) defining their collective identity (which has become increasingly important, as population encroachment from the city of Guadalajara brings more and more outsiders into Jocotán); (2) preserving their folk religious beliefs and practices; and (3) learning to negotiate within the existing social-political power structure while also developing new structures more responsive to indigenous concerns.

Festival Scholarship

Throughout Mexico, fiestas are among the most visible features of life in both urban and rural communities. Most are large celebrations dedicated to the worship of a particular saint or to the commemoration of an important religious event. Whether religious or secular, fiestas typically feature feasting, drinking, and dancing as integral to the celebration. Furthermore, fireworks, candles, flowers, costumes, and other objects are commonly employed during fiestas. Consequently, the staging of such elaborate and complex celebrations requires a considerable expenditure of time, money, and other resources. The religious and socioeconomic complexity of fiestas clearly suggests their importance to anthropologists interested in cultural meaning and significance.

A fundamental premise of this book is that the complex nature of these events demands a comprehensive examination of specific festivals as they are practiced in specific communities, in order to appreciate the many ways in which a given festival may intersect with other areas of social and cultural life. To my knowledge, a comprehensive study of a single festival has not been conducted within the Mexican context to date. Instead, because festival involves many aspects of life, such as religion, identity, tradition, beliefs, and culture change, it has been implicated in a number of anthropological studies of Mexico.[7] In fact, it is difficult to identify even one ethnographic study of Mexico that ignores festival altogether. Hence, although studies of religious festivals have been staples in Mexican ethnography for several decades, most of these have been embedded in larger ethnographic projects. As a result, the existing literature concerning Mexican festival — a literature too complex to adequately address here — reveals divergent interests and perspectives. In order to situate my study theoretically and methodologically, however, in what follows, I shall highlight particular trends within the Mexican festival literature that influenced my thinking as I conceptualized my project.

Until recently, anthropologists have focused almost exclusively on rural communities in which ethnic, class, and rural/urban distinctions appear more rigid and obvious.[8] Under such conditions, anthropologists tended to develop oppositional modes (old/new, capitalist/anticapitalist, Indian/European) as explanatory models, each of which was imbued with a set of static traits. Explicitly or implicitly, the "Indian" community was distinguished on the basis of dress, language, low socioeconomic status, and physical and social isolation, as well as participation in religious festivals. Undoubtedly, such cases represent "ideal" types that do not fully correspond even to the lived reality of the communities they describe; in urban settings, such as Jocotán, however, a complex process of blurring, or hybridization, has resulted from years of constant negotiation between what were originally two distinct systems, making such static models wholly inadequate for grasping the complexities of everyday realities. Moreover, by focusing on communities in rural areas of Mexico identified *a priori* as "Indian," such studies generally overlook the issue of identity as a problem requiring ethnographic investigation, and incidentally help perpetuate the notion that Indians inhabit only rural, not urban sites. In this regard, Friedlander's 1975 study of the meaning of *"indio"* in Hueyapan offered an important corrective to this tendency and forcefully called attention to the need for further anthropological study on Indian identity. Subsequent studies by Brandes (1988), Warren (1978), and Watanabe (1992) have contributed significantly to this endeavor.[9]

Second, much anthropological attention concerns festival sponsorship, with a particular focus on the civil-religious cargo system.[10] Indeed, since the cargo system constitutes a distinctive formal characteristic of Indian communities in colonial Mexico, its persistence today suggests the indigenous roots of a community. And yet, the cargo system varies in time and space, so that in some Mexican communities it has disappeared altogether, while in others it has been revitalized only recently (DeWalt 1975; Rus and Wasserstrom 1980). The cargo system has generated anthropological interest for another reason as well. Since traditional fiestas are typically sponsored by and for the community, resources for the production of fiestas must be found within the community.[11] This concern over resources has provoked a long-standing debate over the economic and political implications of festival.[12] For instance, some scholars have concluded that festivals serve the hegemonic order as a means of socially controlling subordinate indigenous communities because fiestas consume local resources that keep participants from working in other activities to effect political or social change. While these studies call attention to the latent functions of festival sponsorship, their narrow focus on sponsorship results in serious limitations. Within that perspective, the possibility that participants may employ festivals as forums for the articulation and advancement of competing political agendas is not fully considered.[13] Moreover, without a full treatment of the festival, we have no understanding concerning what motivates individuals to participate in the festival. Finally, focusing too narrowly on the cargo system may obscure important dynamics, such as reciprocity and networking, that have economic implications and are fundamental in motivating the festival cycle.

Another important body of Mexican festival scholarship deals with ritual humor and/or symbolic reversals in the festival context.[14] Among the most significant contributions generated from this scholarship is the idea that different modes of communication may be strategically employed to convey covert or contestative messages. These studies, in particular, have greatly inspired and influenced my own understanding of Mexican fiestas.

Two common features within these three trends may be noted. First and foremost, they do not provide a comprehensive coverage of a single festival. And, with notable exceptions, especially among some of the more recent studies, they tend to espouse a static view of society that does not fully account for social change or differential power relations within a group.

In part, these characteristics reflect the dominant trends in anthropology at the time during which the work was conducted. In particular, functionalist theory, which dominated the field from the 1930s to the 1960s, appears to have been especially influential in the study of festivals, not only in Mexico, but elsewhere around the world. Commenting on the widespread usage of functionalist theory, Eisenstadt notes that anthropologists working within this approach

showed how these festivals served, by representing or portraying the common symbols of the society and by bringing different sectors of the society together in a festival and highly emotional ritual solidarity, as integrative mechanisms, alleviating the society's tensions. (1990, 244)

The functionalist approach became especially attractive because it provided an explanation for that which seemed irrational. For instance, by assuming that groups would inevitably, if unconsciously, work to maintain social cohesion, the functionalist approach explained why individuals participated in the fiestas even when participation demanded many more resources than they could afford. However, functionalist theory could not adequately account for social change or differential power relations within a group, and therefore further reinforced the concept of identity as a fixed and static category.

Within the existing literature on Mexican festival, Stanley Brandes's book *Power and Persuasion* (1988) most closely approximates the treatment of festival I propose. Not only does he focus on a regional area that has not received much attention with respect to festival studies, but he also explores many important issues such as state intervention and exploitation of local festivals, identity, and exchange. Furthermore, Brandes's stated objective is to illustrate how festivals serve as a means of regulating controlling processes. Read optimistically, his study provides a look at how festival is an important arena for the negotiation of power both within the local community and in relation to the Mexican state. In these respects, Brandes's work represents a refreshing and much needed departure from past studies. Yet, because his analyses are framed within the functionalist notion of festival as an agent of social control, and because no particular fiesta is treated in full detail, we are left wanting a more extended and comprehensive understanding of festival.

My study of La Fiesta de los Tastoanes in Jocotán addresses these issues and ameliorates the previously mentioned limitations in several ways. Unlike other studies that have focused primarily on remote indigenous communities, I focus on Jocotán, which is an ancient, indigenous community situated alongside the second largest city in Mexico. The geographical location of Jocotán brings into sharp relief rural/urban borders, boundaries of identity, and distinctions between modern and traditional as points of conflict and tension that demand attention. I also employ the concept of hegemony to provide a more holistic understanding of one festival. Unlike the functionalist approach, the concept of hegemony not only allows for contested meanings of the festival in the community over time but, more importantly, calls attention to those dynamics that invest the festival with meaning. Although I focus on contemporary Jocotán, I also provide a historical perspective to detail the way La Fiesta de los Tastoanes has been used in the struggle over hegemony from the Spanish conquest to the present.

This study is organized as follows: Chapter 1 describes the festival as it is presently performed in Jocotán and provides the reader with an overview of the characters, the plot, and the sequence of activities. Chapter 2 explores the relationship between knowledge, experience, and gender as these emerged in my fieldwork experience, and thus provides an opportunity to introduce the community as I encountered it on my extended visit in 1986. Chapter 3 sketches the history of Jocotán from the preconquest era to the present, noting significant forces that have contributed to the difficult political and economic position in which Jocoteños now find themselves. And Chapter 4 provides a descriptive account of contemporary Jocotán.

Chapter 5 explores the local legend upon which the Tastoanes festival is based as a politically charged discourse concerning power and domination. Chapter 6 investigates the issue of reciprocity, especially as it is manifested in the *prenda* system, to illustrate obscure, yet critical, aspects of the festival. Chapter 7 examines the strategy of hybridization as it is employed and articulated in the festival. With a focus on the children, Chapter 8 examines the impact of institutional forces in Mexico that constitute the dominant culture upon forms of local culture. Finally, in addition to summarizing the main points elaborated in the previous chapters, Chapter 9 offers general conclusions regarding the significance of the Tastoanes festival in present-day Jocotán and places my analytical findings in the theoretical context of contemporary festival analysis.

ONE

The Festival Performance

A Description

I awoke to the sound of music: banda music blasting me out of my sleep at — I looked at my watch on the nightstand — 5 a.m.! Suddenly, I realized this was no radio alarm, it was the mañanitas for Santiago, announcing the official beginning of La Fiesta de los Tastoanes. I dressed hurriedly and ran to the church.

I had been told about las mañanitas, but never having experienced it in my previous visits, I assumed that it no longer took place. Perhaps it once had, long ago, I thought, but today, it's probably too much trouble or too expensive. When I had heard the people of Jocotán describe it, I figured they were probably indulging in nostalgic recollections of the past. On this point, I was wrong.

At the church, as I hurriedly snapped various shots of the musicians, I couldn't help but feel self-conscious: after all, I must have looked pretty funny with my unruly hair announcing to everyone that I had just woken up — not a very professional image for someone who had come all the way from the United States to study the fiesta. I also felt self-conscious recording the event on film, for it underscored that I was ultimately preparing data for an outside audience, in effect gathering evidence to substantiate my authority to represent the people of Jocotán as a first-hand "eyewitness."[1] In retrospect, I see that my discomfort stemmed from all of that but also — and most of all — from the fact that I had not believed what the Jocoteños had told me until I saw for myself.

On my first visit to Jocotán, I was overwhelmed by the complexities of the festival. I tried to capture the various components of the festival on camera and on paper, as well as on audio- and videotape, but it seemed chaotic and I had a hard time following the story line and understanding what was going on. Grasping all the nuances and achieving an understanding of the "whole" festival remains a constant challenge, for by its very nature the festival is dynamic, subject to change at numerous levels. So I listened carefully to what the people in the crowds were telling each other, and I slowly started to engage in these conversations, asking my own questions and gradually formulating my own opinions and interpretations. Over the years, I have come to understand that the ongoing dialogue between the participants and the audience during the performance constitutes an important aspect of the interpretative process.

In striking ways, my experience of the Tastoanes festival resonates with Kenneth Burke's notion of history as an unending conversation in which participants enter at specific moments in time (1941). Burke asks the reader to imagine a conversation taking place in a parlor. Arriving late, one encounters a heated debate, and once one has heard enough to get a sense of the issues, one engages in the conversation, offering opinions and formulating attitudes (1941, 110–11). Burke's statement suggests two key points: (1) that there is no such thing as "historical truth" or "objectivity," but rather that history is the interpretation of the past presented from a particular point of view and for particular reasons; and (2) people draw upon an experience or situation from the past that serves as a metaphor for expressing, and thus understanding, their current situation. Regarding the second point, Burke claims that such experiences or situations in life constitute the basis for the development of dramatic or symbolic acts. These acts may be verbal, taking some recognized narrative form such as legend or myth, or they may be communicated through action, as in a play, for instance. Rooted in life experience, such creative works encompass common or recurring situations and embody attitudes towards that situation.

Burke's insight on dramatic and creative work has contributed significantly to the study of cultural process and performance. First, he calls attention to the issue of subjectivity in any act of interpretation, an idea that scholars have recently taken up.[2] Second, he emphasizes that collective attitudes toward certain situations are encompassed within a dramatic or symbolic act, an idea currently promoted by cultural performance theorists.[3] I find Burke's contributions useful for comprehending the complex nature of La Fiesta de los Tastoanes. In particular, that (1) the initial encounter between the Spaniards and the Mexican natives has generated multiple interpretations; (2) the festival not only constitutes a collective attitude toward that encounter but may also serve as a metaphor for understanding present situations in Jocotán today; and (3) with each performance, the fiesta generates new interpretations about the past and its links to the present. These multiple interpretations about the Spanish/indigenous encounter take the form of historical narratives (legends, stories, texts) and dramatic performances.

Since humans communicate what they know and believe about past experiences and events in countless ways, making use of all senses, historical knowledge is not confined to written accounts.[4] Yet, Western scholars have tended to privilege written accounts, dismissing oral forms of documenting history as insignificant, untenable, or otherwise inferior. For instance, oral or performative accounts of the past are typically labeled "myths," meaning untrue, whereas the written record is presumed to be "objective" and therefore "accurate." But, as Burke and others have noted, history is not reducible to "what really happened" and, thus, perceptions of the past are inevitably multiple, partial, and subjective.[5] Hence, the issue of subjectivity extends into the official or scholarly historical texts as well as to oral, local, or unofficial stories. Significantly, each recounting of a given event explicitly or implicitly promotes a particular version or point of view. In writing this book, I struggled to determine how to make sense of the complex nature of La Fiesta de los Tastoanes. Which of the many stories contained in, and told about, the festival would I and should I tell? In which order should I present my "facts"? What position(s) should I take or assume?

I decided that the very first step in this analysis must be to provide a general description of the festival itself. Then, in subsequent chapters, I tell the less well-known stories concerning the initial Spanish–indigenous encounter — stories rooted in the community, developed in and around the festival, and based on my own experience, rather than those recorded in official texts and promoted through state or religious institutions.[6]

The following account is a reconstruction based on my extended visit in 1986 with details filled in from my observations made over the past ten years. While the constitutive elements of the festival remain fairly constant from one year to the next, each performance is unique. This reconstruction is intended to provide the reader with a general understanding of the structure of participation, the cast of characters, and the sequence of activities, in order to better follow my analysis in later chapters.

Festival Participants

Participation in La Fiesta de los Tastoanes is virtually open to everyone, but the opportunity to assume the role of a character in the drama is limited almost exclusively to males approximately 15 years or older. In this way, males acquire more experience in performance over time, and, therefore, elder men typically occupy the leading roles. The characters of the drama are divided into two groups: the Spanish Christians and the Tastoanes.

Leading the Spanish Christians, Santiago wears three special items—a hat trimmed with ribbon and feathers, a *dengue* or band draped across his chest, and silver spurs on his boots. He also carries a large silver sword, which he uses freely. Most importantly, Santiago rides a horse (representing his brother Jacob) whose blanket is trimmed in gold and around whose neck is also draped a dengue, to match Santiago's outfit. Santiago's elaborate costume, his free use of the sword, and, above all, the fact that he is the only horseman, signal his superior status.

Santiago's *ayudantes*, or assistants, who protect Santiago and maintain order in the festival at all times, include *El Moro* (the Moor), *El Sargento* (the Sergeant), and *El Perrito Rastrero* (the Hound Dog). The relationship between Santiago and his ayudantes is manifested primarily in three ways. First, the ayudantes wear simplified versions of Santiago's costume, consisting of a feathered hat and a brightly colored dengue across their chests. Second, since their principal task is to defend and protect Santiago, they enjoy free use of their swords, that is, they may strike their opponents with their swords. Finally, in their role as ayudantes, they must be prepared to substitute for Santiago at any given point during the festival should the need arise (e.g., in the event that Santiago is injured or needs a break). Thus, although they do not mount a horse throughout the entire festival, as does Santiago, they do have limited access to Santiago's horse. They also share other features with Santiago: they all speak Spanish, none of them wears a mask, and they are Christian. Thus, the qualities that characterize the Spanish Christians include: Spanish culture, their role as conquerors, the Spanish language, Christianity, horsemanship, seriousness, authority, and a strict hierarchical structure.

The Tastoanes constitute a more complex group since they are further divided into at least three sub-groups: the reyes, Cyrineo, and the general corps of Tastoanes. Three *reyes*, or kings—Herodes, Anás, and Pilatos— serve as the primary spokesmen for the Tastoanes and act as the official leaders of the Tastoanes group, though they do not actively engage in the battles. Instead, they stand on the sidelines and function as supervisors and counselors. To emphasize their nonviolent roles, the reyes rarely even carry a sword, preferring instead a *burrita de otate* (a bamboo cane with a carved handle that resembles a donkey face), which is never used as a weapon. Furthermore, they wear mid-length, green dresses (worn over pants), a pink cape, a Tastoanes mask, and braids, thus suggesting female personas.[7] In dress, attitude, and action, the reyes symbolically invert what Santiago represents. They are female — or at least transvestites — nonviolent, and opposed to Christianity.

Cyrineo plays a unique role within the Tastoanes category. He is the only Tastoan who befriends Santiago. His ambiguous character is reflected in his costume and behavior. Wearing the mask of a white man and dressed in a red suit reminiscent of a court jester, Cyrineo visually stands apart from both groups. Cyrineo's mask merits special attention, in light of the fact that even Santiago and his helpers, who represent white men, wear no masks at all. Furthermore, in the dramatic performance Cyrineo vacillates between remaining loyal to the Tastoanes and befriending Santiago, and ultimately brings Santiago to his death. As this suggests, Cyrineo is an anomalous character who has no well-defined loyalties. His lack of loyalty to either the protagonists or the antagonist marks Cyrineo as the ultimate danger, ambivalence. Indeed, Cyrineo may ultimately represent the folly of attempting to become the "other" simply by making superficial changes.

The general corps of Tastoanes dress in dark jackets (similar to sports jackets) called *levas* and each wears a pair of bright *calzoncillos*, or shorts, over dark pants. However, the most impressive feature of their costume is a multicolored leather mask with the face of a fear-inspiring, animal-like creature, topped with long, stringy, straw-like hair. In addition, the Tastoanes use a special language consisting of indigenous, Spanish, and nonsense words. Often, they communicate using sheer gibberish and making animal-like sounds, such as grunts and howls.

The foolish babbling and the animal-like masks may be explained in several ways. According to historical sources, at the time of the conquest the Mexican natives employed these as strategies to scare off their opponents. However, the Spanish conquerors simply "read" this as another indication of the natives' "uncivilized" state (other signs included pagan beliefs, scant clothing, and polygamous relationships). Another possibility is that the "gibberish" alludes to the communication problems experienced on both sides during the initial encounter, a situation that made the use of gestures and pantomime indispensable strategies for communication. In the festival context, the use of animal masks and sounds may be explained by the fact that this is one of various forms employed by ritual clowns to challenge the social order. Indeed, the behavior of the Tastoanes coincides directly with the overt and intense licentious festival behavior typical of ritual clowns. As the term licentiousness implies, ritual clowns assert their virtually total freedom to play with social categories and cultural order by employing the principles of juxtaposition, novelty, condensation, exaggeration, inversion, and humor. Examples of festival behavior include excessive drinking, cross-dressing, and indulging in prankish acts (Hieb 1979; Willeford 1969; Norbeck 1978; Bauman and Abrahams 1978; Bricker 1973; and Crumrine 1967).

The antics of the Tastoanes demand courage, wit, and the cooperation of all members of this group. As a whole, the Tastoanes (including the reyes and Cyrineo) are *peones*, or peons, in the most literal sense, that is, they are not allowed to ride on horseback. Their subordinate position to the Spanish Christians is further reinforced by the fact that although the Tastoanes outnumber their adversaries and are armed with swords, they are not allowed to physically or directly strike their opponents.[8] Yet, Santiago and his helpers can and do strike the Tastoanes. For this reason, the main objective for the Tastoanes is to literally and metaphorically knock Santiago off his "high" horse — the ultimate humiliation for Santiago — by relying solely on their quick wit, humor, and cooperative team effort. They accomplish this mainly by causing Santiago to lose his temper and his self-control, as well as his control over his horse, Jacob. For example, the Tastoanes may poke or jab at the horse to scare it into bucking Santiago off, or they may taunt Santiago into chasing them until he loses control of Jacob. The spectators cheer with excitement every time the Tastoanes rile Santiago, and whoever succeeds in actually making Santiago fall off the horse is rewarded with a jug of *huariche*, which is a local term for hard liquor, usually mescal or tequila.

Of all the characters, Santiago plays the most important role, for although all participants must help organize the festival, the person playing the role of Santiago remains the principal festival sponsor. Santiago's responsibilities begin on the last day of the festival one year and continue until the end of the second day of the festival the following year. During that one-year period, he must prepare and organize the community to ensure that the festival is celebrated properly. Additionally, Santiago must pay for all festival activities during his term, although in private he may (and typically does) receive economic assistance from close friends or family members.

Santiago relies heavily on his family members, especially his wife, to assist him with certain aspects of the festival. The women in the family (wife, daughters, sisters, mothers) provide the labor and skills to successfully complete the numerous tasks required in the festival. For instance, they make special costumes for the actor and for the statue of Santiago in the church, often making identical outfits for both. They also clean and decorate the church for the festival. But the largest task involves preparing and serving the food for the festival luncheon. Since the entire community and all outside guests may attend the luncheons, the luncheons require a great deal of time and energy. Usually the cooking begins several days before the festival.

Other participants in the festival include the prenda volunteers, the musicians, and, of course, the spectators. The word *prenda* means token or offering and refers to special gifts for Santiago. Each year, seven individuals volunteer to receive the gifts for Santiago, with the understanding that they must present gifts of equal or greater value the following year. No explicit restrictions dictate who may or may not be a volunteer; however, preference is given to those individuals who must pay a *manda*, or sacred vow, and, all things being equal, preference is usually given to long-time residents of Jocotán. The complex prenda system figures centrally in the Jocoteño version of the Tastoanes festival. Because it constitutes its most distinctive feature, I provide a detailed discussion on the subject in Chapter 6.

Like the prenda volunteers, the musicians contribute significantly to the dynamics of La Fiesta de los Tastoanes, for they perform throughout the entire festival period. Although the chirimía originated in Europe, it has since become associated primarily with indigenous musical practices throughout Latin America, especially when accompanied by the *tambor*, or drum. Indeed, the chirimía-and-drum ensemble figures centrally in the Tastoanes festival because the melodies they play cue certain actions. Musicians from neighboring communities often fill this important role when local musicians are unavailable.

Brass bands, or *bandas*, commonly found in all mestizo areas of Latin America, also play an important role in La Fiesta de los Tastoanes.[9] Generally, this ensemble consists of at least one or two trumpets, a saxophone, a snare drum, and a bass drum, although other instruments may be added. In La Fiesta de los Tastoanes, several bandas play for Santiago at dawn on the first day of the festival. This is called *llevando las mañanitas*, or serenading the saint. After that, the brass bands do not perform again until the close of the festival, usually during the final procession and at the closing dance.

Spectators comprise another important aspect of the festival; whether they support it or not, most community members watch the festival at some point. Some people stop to gaze for a few minutes and then go on with their routine business, while others stay to watch for hours at a time. The number of spectators fluctuates, depending primarily on the particular event taking place: peak moments of dramatic activity always draw a large audience. The festival attracts spectators from surrounding towns as well, and visitors from those communities where a Tastoanes festival is also held inevitably make comparisons to their own festival.

Spectators represent all age groups, but it is the children who make up the single largest group of spectators. In fact, many of the children make special masks out of milk cartons to wear for the festival and to play "Tastoanes" on the sidelines or at home. Children make up many games based on the Tastoanes festival, but the general idea is that one child will ride a stick or branch as a horse while the others will try to knock him down and take his place on the "horse." The consistent presence of children in festival activities warrants special attention and is taken up in Chapter 8.

Unlike the eager children, the priest of the community requires substantial encouragement to participate in La Fiesta de los Tastoanes. Each morning the priest must officiate mass before the jugadas begin, and he must celebrate mass at the closing ceremony. In addition, his permission is required in order to use the church, the atrium, and the statue of Santiago. His cooperation is critical to the successful performance of the festival. (See Chapter 7 for a detailed discussion of the priest.)

Having outlined the cast of characters and the structure of participation, I will now turn to the sequence of activities.

Sequence of Events

August 15 marks the first official day of festival activities for the year. In the evening, the individual performing the role of Santiago holds a meeting at which male participants of the festival gather to organize the Tastoanes festival for the year. As the sun sets, a small group of men set out on foot to advertise the organization meeting scheduled for that evening. Accompanied by the chirimía and tambor players, the men engage in smalltalk and light drinking as they circulate through the town, stopping at each home where festival participants live. At each stop, the musicians play briefly while one of the men knocks on the door to invite the residents to participate in the festival that year. While many family members greet this growing procession, only the men of the household receive invitations to partake of liquor and join the procession. As the evening wears on, the group gets bigger and louder. Many people stand at their doorways and windows to watch as the group travels around the town, and many children cannot resist the temptation to join in the fun. For this occasion, many children wear their milk-carton masks, even though adults do not dress in costume. In addition to following the procession, children play various "Tastoanes" games throughout the community.

By the time the procession returns to Santiago's house, the crowd may have become quite unruly. Once inside, the men discuss such things as who will play the role of Santiago next year, who has to submit a prenda, and what precautionary measures must be taken to maintain a good and safe festival. Since the men have been drinking quite a bit by this time, the discussions can quickly turn into arguments, but once everyone has had his say, they all remind each other that for the saint's sake they have to keep the festival going and therefore must reach a consensus (see Chapter 6 for a detailed example). During the meeting, *atole*, a thick porridgelike warm beverage, and *birote*, a type of French bread, are served to everyone, and this food seems to help people maintain or regain their sobriety. By midnight, the meeting officially ends. Although some participants may continue talking or drinking far into the night, others simply go home to sleep.

On September 8 the dramatic action of the festival begins. Even before the sun rises, the bandas greet Santiago (represented by his statue in the church) with *Las Mañanitas*,[10] announcing to everyone that La Fiesta de los Tastoanes has begun. Besides the traditional saint's day song, the bandas serenade Santiago with *cumbias* and *rancheras*, secular song and dance tunes associated with Mexican popular culture. Although these melodies may seem unconventional, if not profane, they appear much more appropriate as personal expressions than the sanctioned church hymns.

Inside the already decorated church waits Santiago (the statue), elegantly dressed and placed on a decorated platform in front of the altar. Slowly, the faithful arrive, some bringing flowers and candles to place around the statue while others bring small children dressed either as Tastoanes or as Santiago to pay a manda; still others simply stop by to pay their respects. Exchanging *saludos*, the devotees mill around outside to enjoy the music and observe the steady stream of new arrivals. After about an hour, the music ends, signaling to the festival participants that breakfast, which is hosted each day by a different family, will begin shortly. However, since only those individuals playing a character role in the festival attend the breakfast, the activity around the church continues until 9 a.m., when the morning mass begins.

Despite the fact that the mass is dedicated by the community to Santiago, the priest usually does not mention Santiago or the Tastoanes festival during mass. Nevertheless, Jocoteños employ other markers to indicate that this special mass is offered in Santiago's honor. Santiago's devotees fill the church well beyond capacity, and many of the Tastoanes attend mass dressed in costume. But perhaps the biggest marker is the handsomely decorated image of Santiago himself, moved from its niche along the lateral wall inside the church to occupy a prominent place in front of the altar. Semiotically, placing Santiago in front of the altar makes a strong statement, in that it inverts the concept of "idols behind altars," thus affirming the conscious decision of the Jocoteños to openly assert their religious beliefs.

After mass, some of the Tastoanes begin dancing around in the church atrium, but many prefer to follow Santiago (the man playing the role) as he goes from house to house gathering the main performers. This procession resembles the one held on August 15 in that the excitement and noise increase as more and more participants join Santiago. However, this time, participants appear in full costume. Once again, many young children wear their milk-carton masks and use sticks to imitate the Tastoanes as they follow them in the rowdy procession.

By mid-morning, a crowd has gathered at the churchyard waiting for the drama to unfold. People chat amiably as the performers interact freely with one another as well as with the spectators. Around eleven o'clock, the Tastoanes line up side by side, holding their swords vertically in front of their bodies. Santiago's helpers run by the line and strike the Tastoanes' swords with their own to ensure that the Tastoanes maintain order. This activity is repeated several times, and during the intervals, the Tastoanes dance freely, making grunting noises and hitting each other's swords.

Amidst an expectant crowd, the dramatic plot unfolds, as the head Tastoan interrogates Santiago concerning his presence in their territory and his intentions there. The reyes order the Tastoanes to measure and outline their territory (an event called *midiendo la mojonera* and *partiendo plaza*), a task they perform by going to each corner of the square block on which the church is located. A small crowd follows the group into the street, but an even larger crowd waits at the churchyard for their return, going from one side of the churchyard to the other to see as much of the drama as possible.

At each corner, the Tastoanes argue fiercely with Santiago and his assistants for about ten minutes. Part of this text consists of memorized lines, but since most of the lines have long been forgotten, each actor must improvise.[11] Because of the leather masks worn by the Tastoanes, their voices sound muffled, making it difficult to understand all they say, and the fact that part of the dialogue consists of nonsense words makes it even worse. To communicate more effectively, the Tastoanes rely on the intonation of their voices and exaggerated body expressions to reveal their anger and frustration. Taking their cue from the chirimía and drum ensemble, who play specific tunes to signal the performers, the Tastoanes dance for a short period and then move on to the next corner. At the fourth corner the argument intensifies momentarily, hinting at the inevitable outbreak of violence.

Once back in the church atrium, before an even larger crowd, the Tastoanes begin a heated discussion with Cyrineo. Cyrineo alternates between arguing and ringing the church bells. While he does the latter, the Tastoanes engage in a mock sword-fight dance with each other. Then, around twelve o'clock, in response to Cyrineo's call, Santiago arrives and immediately the Tastoanes surround him. Two Tastoanes begin sharpening their swords, and within a short time, Santiago is stabbed and his body is laid out on the ground and covered with a blanket. Bananas, apples, guavas, and other fruits are placed beneath the blanket to represent Santiago's internal organs. Overcome with grief and remorse at having lured Santiago to his death, Cyrineo throws himself on the corpse and weeps loudly and bitterly. He runs back and forth from Santiago's body to the church entrance, where he rings the bells again. In an effort to revive Santiago, Cyrineo sweeps Santiago's body with a branch, but his efforts are useless.[12]

By this time, the churchyard has become packed with spectators anxious to see the action, so Santiago's helpers — El Moro, El Sargento, and El Perrito Rastrero — must continually push them back to make room for the performance. At the same time, the helpers have to guard against the Tastoanes, who sneak up to the corpse to prematurely snatch the pieces of fruit representing Santiago's organs. Sometimes the helpers grab the Tastoanes by the hair, yanking them back in line, or else they chase and hit them with their swords.

While all this is going on, the musicians play a solemn tune with an extended drum cadence appropriate for a military funeral. However, laughter interrupts the solemnity of the occasion, as Santiago, who is supposed to be dead, begins to smoke a cigarette or to eat some of the fruit placed upon him. Herodes, one of the kings, lifts the blanket, examines the corpse, and with the help of a Tastoan, pretends to cut up the body as if he were slicing beef, using exaggerated motions to express his great pleasure.

The only serious performers, besides the musicians, are Santiago's helpers, who must control both the crowd and the Tastoanes. Under the intense heat created by the hot midday sun and the smothering crowds, the helpers, who have become the butt of the Tastoanes' pranks, become so irritated that they strike fiercely at the Tastoanes. But the taunting Tastoanes only continue to show off their bravery by antagonizing the helpers even further, to the delight of the spectators.

One of the elder Tastoanes assists the kings in taking all the remaining fruit from Santiago's body, but as they throw it out to El Perrito Rastrero, the spectators rush forward to intercept. Santiago then gets up and begins to march up and down the entrance to the church, flanked by one of his assistants and Cyrineo. Cyrineo holds Santiago's hat on a pole directly in front of Santiago, which seems to indicate that Santiago's presence is spiritual rather than physical.

When Santiago finally leaves, the Tastoanes make a large circle, extending their arms out to each other with a sword in the right hand so that the swords act as links between them. Cyrineo and Santiago's assistants ceremoniously enter the circle. Santiago arrives shortly, riding Jacob once again, and joins his allies inside the circle. He swings his sword in the air, making a sign of the cross, and the Tastoanes fall to the ground. Then his assistants go around tapping the Tastoanes' swords with their own to restore life to the fallen Tastoanes. Thus, the Tastoanes are reborn through the powers of Santiago.

At this point, the performers usually break for a luncheon, which is served at Santiago's house. Large tables are set up everywhere — in the patio, in the street — to accommodate the large crowds that come to eat. In addition to the performers, it is primarily other men and children who attend the luncheon; virtually the only adult women present are those serving the food.

During the luncheon the men relax and joke, and the unmasked and semi-costumed performers compare cuts and bruises received in "battle." The conflicts enacted in the drama are not in evidence here, as everyone eats, drinks, and relaxes for two hours or more, regaining the energy and spirit to go into battle once again.

In mid-afternoon a series of jugadas takes place at various locations around town and these continue until sundown. The locations for these mock confrontations are usually chosen on the basis of the comfort they provide for the performers and the spectators. Shaded areas, for example, provide protection from the scorching sun, allowing the audience to watch for longer periods and the performers to tire less quickly. Sometimes a family will request a performance in front of their house, usually in honor of a deceased family member who used to participate in the Tastoanes festival. When this occurs, special friends and family gather at that house to watch the performance for a while. By sundown, the jugadas stop, the crowd disperses, and the festival activities end for the day.

The festivities begin slowly the second day. The Tastoanes start their day with a breakfast sponsored by one of the families, and mass begins around

9 a.m. All day long the Tastoanes and Santiago engage in jugadas at different sites around Jocotán. As on the previous day, the skirmishes cease temporarily when the musicians play a special tune signaling the Tastoanes to perform a choreographed war dance.

The dance features only the Tastoanes, who form two opposing lines, meet face-to-face with a partner, hit their swords against their partner's sword, and cross to the other side. Then, the person on the extreme right of each line runs to the opposite line and hits the swords of all the opponents in that line with his own sword. He then runs back to his own line, standing now on the left end. Each person in line repeats this pattern until everyone is back to his original position.

After the lunch recess at Santiago's house, the dancing and fighting may resume for a short period. But the major event of the afternoon is the *entrega de las prendas*, or the presentation of special offerings. Santiago has a list of the seven volunteers who must provide the prendas and he sends out small groups of Tastoanes and his helpers to pick up the prenda from each volunteer's house. The prendas are then brought to Santiago's house — unless he happens to live in "la zona," across the boulevard, in which case the gifts are taken to the church. A huge crowd gathers at the site where the gifts are displayed, commenting freely on the quality of the prendas.

Once all the prendas have been gathered, Santiago proceeds to distribute them among the "new" volunteers, that is, the volunteers for the next year's festival. Finally, with great ceremony, Santiago removes his hat, spurs, and sword and gives them to the new Santiago, who will assume his duties as of that moment. Often, the Tastoanes and the new Santiago engage in several jugadas that afternoon to *estrenar*, or break in, the new Santiago. But for most people, this marks the end of the festivities for the day.

On the third and final day, a healing ritual brings closure to the festival. After a breakfast and a mass, jugadas and dancing continue all day, breaking only for lunch at the new Santiago's house. The culminating event of the day, and the highlight of the festival as a whole, occurs late in the afternoon, around five o'clock. A solemn procession, beginning at the church, circulates through the entire town, increasing steadily in size as it heads back to the church. The core unit of the procession consists of the characters of the drama, in or out of costume. Santiago, riding Jacob and surrounded by several Tastoanes, heads the procession. Following closely behind are two men carrying a decorated platform on which stands the statue of Santiago. They are accompanied by four other men holding a large golden canopy over them and preceded by two more men, one carrying an elevated cross and the other carrying a bell which he rings continuously. All the rest of the cast members surround this second group. Behind them come the rest of the community members.

The procession, though solemn, is a very noisy one. Women, often carrying large floral arrangements, sing hymns of praise in harmonious a cappella melodies. Additional music is provided by the chirimía and tambor ensemble, as well by as the bandas, each playing different songs. Together with the constant sound of the ringing bell, the processional sounds are punctuated by sporadic explosions of skyrockets and firecrackers signaling that a major change is about to occur.

Once they arrive at the church, silence falls upon the processional members. The church fills rapidly, with the rest of the participants assembling in the atrium. The entrance to the church is cleared, and the statue of Santiago is carried to the front of the altar. Meanwhile, Santiago (the actor) and Jacob remain in the churchyard. Then, the Tastoanes, and anyone else who wishes to participate, line up before Santiago, who hits them three or four times with his sword. They then proceed down the church aisle, often on their knees. In front of the altar, the sacristan, using the little sword from the statue of Santiago, hits them on whatever part of the body they request, as many times as they desire. Many people believe that the sword heals any part of the body it touches. Others participate in this ritual as a penance, a manda, or as an expression of their devotion to Santiago.

The festival ends as Santiago dismounts Jacob and enters the church, where he, too, undergoes the ritual executed by the sacristan. In this way, Santiago acknowledges that he is merely a representative of a more powerful force, and he becomes once again a regular Jocoteño. As the climax of the entire festival, the healing ritual assumes a central role, stressing once again its powers of renewal and transformation.

Typically, festivities continue far into the night after all the ritual activities have terminated. Large crowds socialize in the church atrium, while street vendors sell beverages, snacks, and small miscellaneous items such as headbands, balloons, and small toys. Occasionally, a fireworks display entertains the crowd, and often, bands hired to play outside the church inspire people to dance in the streets. For this day, at least, Jocoteños publicly assert their right to inhabit and use their territory as they see fit.

Conclusion

The foregoing description suggests the multiple and complex dimensions of festival that shape perceptions, representations, and authorship of the past. Although particular agents, such as the priest or the *Tastoanes mayores* (i.e., the senior men who have been actively involved in the Tastoanes festival for many generations), may attempt to impose particular views consistent with their own agendas, the fact remains that various meanings become possible through the performance of the festival. Thus, for example, while the Tastoanes mayores supervise the festival and assume the responsibility for remembering how and why it should be performed, anyone who attends the festival in some way participates in the interpretative process. In informal conversations at home, at the preparative event and, above all, throughout the festival performance, observations, commentaries, and questions abound concerning the meaning of the festival and its central themes: the invasion by the Spaniards and the introduction of Catholicism. In sum, the festival generates numerous conversations about the meaning of the past, and in doing so creates space for multiple alternative and contrasting interpretations. In the following chapters, I explore some of these stories.

T W O

Personal Encounters

↓

The principal theme addressed in the festival concerns encounters: the initial encounter between the Spaniards and the Mexican natives; between the Christians and the pagans; between tradition and change; between the old and the new; between the weak and the strong; and even between the anthropologist and the community. These multiple encounters embedded in La Fiesta de los Tastoanes contribute to its symbolic power and complex nature. In this chapter, I tell a story of my experience in the field in order to better explore the issue of positionality as well as to provide the reader with more details about the conditions under which I obtained my data on the festival and the community.

Position, Knowledge, and Experiences in the Field

Conducting ethnographic research poses serious questions concerning the relationship between knowledge, experience, and subjectivity. For instance, the fact that males and females participate in, and thus experience, La Fiesta de los Tastoanes in very different terms suggests that males and females acquire different knowledge about the festival. However, if gender shapes experience, how could I, a woman, access both the female and male perspectives? And, more importantly, what other factors regarding my personal background and social status could or would affect my access to knowledge within the community?

The issue of knowledge has recently surfaced in anthropology in at least two ways: first, anthropologists have increasingly engaged in serious re-theorizing about doing and writing ethnography, implicating questions concerning how knowledge is acquired, constructed, and disseminated.[1] Second, feminist theorists have called attention to the struggle over authority in matters relating to knowledge, both in the field and in academia. Much of this work involves recognizing that "all knowers investigate, interpret and know from a specific standpoint" (Theriot 1990, 4), thereby challenging the notion that only males can be legitimate agents of knowledge. Together, these works cast further doubt on the waning claim to objectivity in the social sciences. Indeed, the general consensus that emerges from these texts is that the production of knowledge is inextricably tied to issues of power and position.

One issue that warrants further attention concerns the role of the native researcher. Generally, anthropologists have conducted field research in areas or communities quite distinct from their own, resulting in little attention to the special situations a native ethnographer might encounter.[2] Although James Clifford mentions that "the indigenous ethnographer" may offer "new angles of vision and depths of understanding," he does not elaborate on this point (1989, 9). Research conducted by scholars in their own culture occupies a special place within anthropology that may illuminate issues of epistemology.[3]

The following account of my field experience contributes to this growing field by exploring the links between my subject position and my research. Raised by immigrant parents in California, speaking only Spanish at home, I grew up identifying as a Mexican, and later, as a Chicana. During my entire childhood, I devoutly practiced Catholicism, and the most significant social ties in my family's life were those consecrated by the Church through the *compadrazgo* system. Outside of the nuclear family, all our immediate relatives, whom we visited regularly, lived in Mexico. I thus shared a general Mexican cultural heritage, religion, and language with my subjects of study. I looked like them, and I understood subtle forms of communication such as certain looks and tones, and witty double-entendres. Still, I was an outsider in many respects. I had no family in Jocotán, I had been raised in the United States, and I was to reside in this community only temporarily.[4]

My claim is that the role of the ethnographer never ceases to be "problematic," in that human position and subjectivity is not determined by a single factor such as ethnicity, gender, status, age, or religion. Hence, one's status in a community is not fixed but constantly changing, depending on a variety of factors. In everyday interactions in the field, as various situations emerge, certain aspects of one's identity become more salient, others more silenced or rendered insignificant. With boundaries continually shifting along various axes (class, gender, age, occupation, religious affiliation, etc.) the "insider/outsider" distinction changes according to the specific context of interaction.

My role as a Chicana female anthropologist afforded me greater latitude in developing relationships in Jocotán, for I drew upon my professional training as well as my cultural upbringing to manage interpersonal encounters. Knowing which factors "counted" more in particular situations allowed me to exercise some control in emphasizing those features that would help cultivate better relationships. In general, Jocoteños came to view me as a bridge between two cultures, not exclusively and sometimes not at all because of my role as an anthropologist, but rather because of my ethnicity and gender.

Through my personal interactions in the field, however, I also became acutely aware that gender was a subject of great concern and tension in this community. My status as a female intersected with my ethnic status in a number of interesting and complex ways, which I explore in this chapter. Indeed, my mere presence in the community became a constant reminder of alternative gender roles and therefore provoked reflection and discussion around this sensitive issue among the townspeople. Thus, while I did not set out to study issues of gender and sex roles specifically, it became immediately apparent that these were issues that I simply could not avoid altogether. I discovered that the way in which gender roles are represented in this festival and in routine daily-life activities did not fully reveal how gender — along with the kinds of power individuals exert and the strategies they develop to negotiate the imposed constraints — is understood by the people of Jocotán.

Living in Jocotán

After approximately six years of sporadic and brief periods of fieldwork in Jocotán (especially around festival time), I looked forward to conducting long-term field research. However, doing so required that I deal with several issues that would greatly affect the nature of my field experience. As Rosaldo has noted, "doing fieldwork involves human feelings as excruciating as they are mundane. It also reveals the terrible asymmetries that separate fieldworker and informant" (1989, 175). This became most apparent in securing a place to live. How could I expect a family to take me into their home? How could I guarantee their privacy and they mine? How would I compensate someone for providing room and board? Would I be expected to submit to household rules or would I be treated as an independent adult? Such were the questions that stirred within me as I prepared to live in Jocotán.

Between 1980 and 1986, I had primarily established ties with the main participants of the festival and their families. However, finding a family to host me presented quite a delicate situation. Since most families in Jocotán are extremely poor and live in overcrowded homes, families understandably found it uncomfortable, if not impossible, to accommodate a stranger. For these reasons, I hesitated to ask families to host me, even though I knew it was the only way I could live in Jocotán.

My principal contact was an older man, native to Jocotán, whose family had a long history of leadership in the festival activities. In addition, Don José owned the local pool hall and had a large family of his own.[5] As a well-known and respected member in the community, Don José could help me gain acceptance into the community, particularly with those active in the festival. I decided to discuss my housing needs with Don José since he knew the community well, hoping that he would either invite me to stay with his family or recommend another suitable family. After listening to my dilemma, he suggested I try the parish house or a hotel right outside Jocotán. Just thinking of the horror my own mother would express were I to live in a cheap hotel was all I needed to determine that the hotel did not present a viable option. Residing in the hotel would further highlight my status as an outside visitor, and, as a married woman living alone, I knew I would be putting my reputation at risk. So I pursued the first lead, already anticipating that the priest would find some excuse to turn me away since he refused to have anything to do with the festival. As I expected, he told me that he had no room for me because his two nieces were living with him and their brother would be coming to join them shortly.

Fortunately, one niece said she knew of a family who might put me up, although she would have to discuss the idea with them first. When I returned a few days later, I found that her friend, Chela, was a woman whom I had never met before because her family was not very actively involved in the Tastoanes festival. Chela owned a store, had a 9-year-old daughter, and at that time, her husband worked as a night watchman. For that reason, the mother and daughter slept together, leaving the daughter's room unused and therefore potentially available for me. This sounded better than any option I could imagine, so I rushed to meet the family.

Chela was not home when I stopped by to introduce myself, but I did meet her sister, who suggested I write to Chela (since I was leaving the country the following day). Over the next six months I wrote several times but received no response and feared this was Chela's way of hinting that I was not welcome.

When I arrived in Guadalajara that summer, I ventured out once more to Jocotán to find out whether or not I had a place to stay. I discovered that Chela had not received my letters (mail service in Jocotán is dreadful) and had been wondering what had happened to me. She told me that as far as she was concerned I could stay with her, although she warned me that I should see the entire house before I made a commitment to stay. She modestly explained that since they were still in the process of completing the home, they had no hot water, in fact, no running water, and they had to bathe using buckets of water. Furthermore, she explained that since she ran the little grocery store, she could not *"atenderme bien,"* that is, attend to my needs (e.g., washing, ironing, cooking). In short, she made it clear that she could not offer me the luxuries I was probably accustomed to in the United States. I responded by explaining that I was used to taking care of my own needs, and that although we did have many modern conveniences in the United States, I had experienced similar living arrangements at my grandparents' home in a small rural town in the northern state of Durango. Furthermore, I stressed that an important part of my work was to experience first-hand their living situation. Therefore, I did not need or expect any special luxuries. In the end, we agreed that I would have the daughter's bedroom basically to myself, that I would prepare my own breakfast and dinner, and that she would provide the midday meal (*la comida fuerte*, or the main meal), in exchange for which I would give her a monthly stipend.[6] A week later, I moved in.

My host family lived in better than average conditions for the Jocotán community. That is, they owned a two-story, two-bedroom home which included a small kitchen, a dining room/living room, a small parlor, and an indoor toilet. They were equipped with modest modern conveniences such as a stove, a refrigerator, a black-and-white television, a consolette, and a wringer-type washing machine. A thin layer of cement covered the dirt floors, over which the family eventually planned to place tile. The bath house was located in the patio next to the outdoor sinks, in which we washed laundry, dishes, and our faces. From a well located outside the kitchen, we hauled heavy buckets of water for our daily needs. The sight of me washing my laundry by hand or carrying the buckets of water often evoked some sympathy and even assistance from onlookers. Their reactions and our interactions in such scenarios ruptured the image of me as an insider, emphasizing instead certain distinctions between "me" and "them." As a professional, I was not expected to work with my hands and yet, ironically, my profession (I insisted) called for participating in their everyday life experience, including doing mundane tasks, difficult though they might be.

The store provided my host family with a steady income, which was supplemented by the husband's income whenever he was employed. His employment was sporadic—for example, he had worked as a night watchman and then worked making furniture in the city. When he was not working outside the home or out hustling for a job, he worked in the store. The family also supported the husband's mother, for whom they had built a one-room house in the back yard. The mother shared this house with another son, and she supplemented her income by selling popcorn and other snacks to children in the afternoons.

Chela's family lived next door and provided a lot of support for her. The family consisted of elderly parents, three adult daughters, and two adolescent granddaughters; Chela's brother and his family lived directly across the street. Two of the daughters (Chela's sisters) helped Chela run the store, and it was never clear to me whether or not they actually received a salary.[7] To me it all seemed so casual, for as far as I could tell, no one clocked in or kept a record of who did what. According to the two sisters, when Chela's third son died (two elder sons had died previously), she became very depressed and needed some distraction. Therefore, they encouraged her to set up the store and promised to help her run the business. Although I felt it inappropriate to inquire about the details of their private business arrangement, it became obvious that the principle of working problems out among the members of the family (especially the females) applied to other domains as well. For instance, in her role as a community-service leader, Chela appointed her sisters, and in lesser roles, her father, husband, and brother, to take charge of special tasks because she knew she could count on her family to work efficiently and effectively with her.

As a stranger in their home, I was treated as a special guest and not as a member of the extended family, but I nonetheless had many opportunities to witness intimate aspects of my host family's life. Through my interactions with the family, it became mutually clear that although my stated objective was to study the festival, my interactions with them would color, to an extent, my perception of the community. That is, they were aware that I not only observed the festival but the people in general and, in particular, my host family. We shared no pretense of "pure" objectivity.

As if to break through the absurdity of the situation, Chela's husband insisted on discussing private and intimate details about his (and often their) life with me. During these awkward moments, I had a difficult time figuring out whether I could and should make excuses to leave. Yet, I realized that, among other things, the husband was testing me, trying to figure out what I was up to, how seriously I took my work, and how he and his family would figure in my study. In fact, he openly told me, "Look, I am not perfect and I am not going to pretend to be someone I am not. But I am honest and it is better that you know me for what I am." In part, I think he wanted me to accept him as a real person rather than to have to play a role during my stay. Furthermore, I think it was his way of letting me know that he was aware that I was studying not only the festival but his family, and him as well.

Perhaps discussing his private affairs made him feel he could ask me similar questions, and although I wanted to be fair, I had to be careful not to get involved in "intimate" discussions that would be considered inappropriate for two adult strangers living under the same roof. I knew that because we were members of the opposite sex, I had to keep a certain physical and social distance from the husband to maintain my respectability. When he drank, he became more aggressive. On these occasions, I found it best to avoid him altogether. Occasionally I arranged to stay with friends in Guadalajara to give the family some privacy, a break from my presence. This arrangement seemed ideal because I could pursue research through contacts and archival resources in Guadalajara as well as take time to reflect on my field experience.

But this solution presented yet another set of problems. Chela's husband often questioned me about my activities in Guadalajara, insinuating that I might be cheating on my husband. However, since he didn't make such accusations directly, I had to respond to his *indirectas* (innuendos) in such a way that he would get the message without my directly confronting him. Conversations of this sort were common and stressful because I was constantly having to respond in such a way that did not offend him. On the other hand, I was forced to make him respect me, especially since I continued to live in his home.

The women I met, especially the ones that I came to know best, openly posed questions about my marriage, family, and career, but their inquiries were neither hostile nor intimidating. Rather, they sincerely wanted to know, in practical terms, how I managed to leave my husband to pursue my research. They asked, didn't he get mad at me for abandoning him? Who cooked and cleaned for him during my absence? When I told them that we shared responsibility for doing household chores and that while I was gone, he simply looked after his own needs, they said it must be wonderful having such a supportive and understanding husband.

The women I dealt with most were very hard workers. In addition to caring for their families and doing housework, many held other jobs such as selling clothes or Tupperware, working as maids, or working in the local factories. A few were actively involved in the community. One of the main differences for women, however, was that although they could (and often had to) work outside their homes, for the most part they remained primarily, and often solely, responsible for cooking, cleaning, and child-rearing.

In spite of their hectic schedules, most women devoted some time to relaxing activities in the afternoons. The women in my immediate surroundings gathered every afternoon in a shaded entrance to the house and store. But even while they passed the time talking to one another, they knitted, crocheted, or worked on some other handicraft project. As they worked, conversation flowed from one topic to the next rather freely, and I found this was a good opportunity for me to elicit their perceptions of marriage, motherhood, birth control, dating, and so on.

Women often mentioned that courtship and marriage patterns had improved over the years. For instance, they told me that traditionally couples married at quite an early age, as young as 13 or 14 for women and 16 for men, but today, women wait until they are older. Reflecting on her early marriage with a man she described as having *un genio* (a bad temper), an elder woman noted that *"que esperanzas que uno le alzara la voz a su marido porque así le iba"* ("a woman wouldn't even dream of raising her voice to her husband because she would get it"). Nowadays, she concluded, marriages were better because women *"no se dejaban"* ("wouldn't passively submit to men's authority"). Another woman, approximately 30 years old and engaged to be married, told us that she keeps her fiancé informed of what she thinks, how she feels, and what she does so that he will know her better as a person and *"para que no ande con celos"* ("so he won't be jealous"). In this way, she hoped to cultivate a better marital relationship.

Officially, a marriage must be sanctioned by the church and state, but free unions are not uncommon, especially among teenagers whose parents do not support an early marriage. In such cases, *"robandose la muchacha,"* or "stealing the girl," is a practice couples employ sometimes to pressure their parents to consent to an early marriage. The priest's judgment notwithstanding, parents do not always give in to such tactics, in hopes of sparing their children from a divorce, which some consider to be a far more serious matter. As one father confided, "*Mejor que se esperen para que después no anden batallando con el divorcio*" ("It's better for them to wait so that they won't have to be dealing with a divorce down the road as well"). Once the couple bears a child, however, official marriage becomes obligatory if they wish to baptize their baby.

Baptism is an important sacrament through which a baby becomes initiated into the Catholic church and through which a family can establish or reinforce important links with another family. The child's parents select a couple to sponsor the baptism ritual officiated by the priest. In this way, the couple and the child's parents become *compadres*, while the sponsoring couple become the *padrinos*, or godparents, of the child. The compadrazgo ritual bonds the participating families together, making them, in effect, members of one another's extended family. Children often demonstrate their affection and respect for their godparents through special gestures, such as kissing their hand, while godparents reciprocate by presenting their godchildren with small gifts on special occasions.

Sharing information of this type proved useful for making comparisons in our lives and seemed relatively harmless. I became extremely anxious, however, when my hosts' 9-year-old daughter, after witnessing many of the intimate conversations among the women, confronted her father, telling him that since her mother managed the store and was in charge of community projects, it was only fair that he help her do the household chores. Overhearing this conversation late one night, I lay in bed worried, almost trembling, at possible outcomes. I feared I might be accused of "brainwashing" his daughter, but instead, he simply asked her why he should be like my husband (whom no one had met at that point). She firmly retorted that my husband helped me do the housework and did his own ironing, which gave me time to pursue a career. The father calmly explained that life was different for them because they lived in a different society. Still, the daughter insisted that because her mother worked hard outside of the home, her father should help her mother with household chores. This time, the father responded by pointing out that he too had a job and that in fact he did do quite a bit around the house, and he proceeded to enumerate the various chores he did do.

In light of this exchange, I worked even harder at disclosing my research objectives to clarify my role. A key question that Jocoteños asked me time and again concerned my motivations for studying the festival. Why did I want to study the festival? What would I do with my findings? For me, answering their questions went beyond explaining my particular research project; it entailed disclosing who I was personally and professionally. In effect, their questions forced me to disclose my "position" with respect to my work and my subjects of study.

One way I attempted to clarify my position was by talking casually about my upbringing, my parents' background, my life with my husband, and my reasons for wanting to become an anthropologist. I wanted both Chela and her husband to know that I had been raised with values and roles similar to their own. My decision to pursue a professional career stemmed from my desire to be able to support myself and my future children without a partner if necessary, and because I truly wanted to know more about our rich Mexican heritage. Regarding the first point, I explained that my father had died when I was eight, forcing my mother to work in the agricultural fields, and later the cannery, in order to support six children. During the summer when we worked picking peas my mother would tell us, "If you don't want to spend the rest of your life in the fields, you better get an education because this is the work left to those without a formal education." My disclosing my personal background allowed Jocoteños to relate to me as a *mejicana*, despite the fact that I had been raised in the United States. The fact that I chose to work with them to discover more about my Mexican heritage (thus placing them in positions of authority), and the fact that my work would contribute to the public knowledge about Mexico (through the publication of the book), seemed to foster their collaboration.

Jocoteños expressed great interest in life in the United States, especially since an increasing number of people, particularly young males, ventured across the border for employment. They found it curious that I could be "so Mexican" even though I was born and raised in the United States. Many people told me quite bluntly that they had expected me to be *chocante* (stuck-up) and to deny my Mexican heritage, and to be wealthy. They perceived *mejicanos del otro lado* (literally, Mexicans from the other side) as not speaking Spanish and wanting to be American (i.e., "Anglo"). Therefore, when I discussed my own background and what it was like growing up as a Mexican across the border, they seemed relieved to learn that individuals could maintain language and cultural values even in an often hostile environment. In many ways, I felt that they viewed me as an extension of themselves, a living example of what future generations of their own family might become (especially since emigrating to the United States was increasingly becoming a necessity for many residents of Jocotán).

As a result, they expressed support of my interest in learning more about Mexican culture and they offered to help me learn as much about the festival and life in Jocotán as possible. Often people would literally come up to me and say, "I hear that you want information on the fiesta," and then proceed to tell me their experiences or give me their opinions. People gave me different kinds of information—about why they participated in the festival, how they learned about the festival, why they did or did not like the festival, how the festival had changed over time, what the festival meant to them, who made the masks, how they got their costumes, what the priest told them about the festival, and how other towns celebrated the Tastoanes festival. I felt as though they wanted to educate me and use me to inform the outside world of their experience and lifestyle, particularly since the newspaper reports always seemed to print misinformation concerning Jocoteños and their festival.[8]

One potential drawback of their enthusiasm to educate me was the possibility that they might emphasize the positive. But each individual had a different perspective regarding the festival, particularly in terms of assessing its positive (and negative) aspects. And so, although people generally behaved diplomatically and discreetly, they nonetheless took advantage of me as their captive audience to be quite candid in order to "set the record straight." Thus, by establishing independent relationships with various individuals of Jocotán, I uncovered subtle nuances in their perceptions of the festival.

The best and easiest relationships for me to establish were with the children. In part, this is because I really enjoy being and working with kids. Furthermore, since the kids are everywhere, they are among the first to notice newcomers. Curious by nature, the children would ask me who I was and what I was doing. Shyer kids would often follow me and wait for me to initiate conversation. Sometimes the older kids reprimanded the younger ones for asking me too many personal questions (their favorite questions concerned my age, my marital status, the number of children I had, what my home town was like, and why was I alone). Getting to know the kids proved valuable because they would tell their families about me and vice versa. Also, since they were around quite a bit, they not only knew all the locals but the local gossip as well. Through the children, I heard about many of the tensions and problems that adults were more cautious about disclosing. For instance, one girl alerted me to maintain my distance from "El Sapo" because of his alleged involvement in black magic. Without providing an elaborate explanation, she stated: "*Dicen que es brujo y que hace muchos males, no te han contado? Pregunta y verás lo que te digo.*" ("They say he's a witch and causes lots of misfortunes. Haven't they told you? Go ask and you'll see what I'm talking about.") Such comments forced me to pursue these allegations discreetly (and to confront my own uneasiness) before accepting El Sapo's invitation to interview him in his home — alone. Furthermore, by "innocently" blurting out such comments in front of adults, the children often forced, or at least provided an opportunity for, adults to offer their views on the subject.

The children also proved valuable in providing access to the homes of individuals I had not met or who were not necessarily active in the festival. When they saw me struggling to photograph the festival in action, a few kids would approach me and say, *"Mire, porqué no se sube a la azotea para que alcanze ver mejor, así como están esos chiquillos"* ("Look, why don't you get up on the roof so you can see better, like those other kids"). I'd look up, and sure enough, a group of kids would already be positioned on the rooftop to catch a bird's-eye view. Cautiously, I'd respond, *"Pues no quiero molestar a los dueños, gracias"* ("Well, you see, I don't want to disturb the owners, thanks"). Inevitably, one would shout, *"No se preocupe, es la casa de mi tío,"* or *"La señora no se enoja, yo le pregunto y verá"* ("Don't worry, that's my uncle's house," or "The lady won't be upset, let me ask her and you'll see"). And then, I was in. On the whole, then, the children contributed to my fieldwork by accompanying me to do interviews, helping me carry my equipment and meet people, helping me understand relationships in the community, and providing me with information, solicited and unsolicited.

My relationship with Don José assured me a status of acceptance and respectability among the adults in the community. Since I had known him for several years, he validated that my research interests were sincere. Aware of the importance of his relationship to me in terms of the community, Don José made special efforts to insure that I was safe while in Jocotán. For instance, when introducing me to potential informants, he presented me as a special guest to residents of Jocotán and therefore requested their cooperation in insuring my safety since I was alone.[9] He invited me to join him at various meetings which were attended exclusively by men but, as his invited guest, the men treated me with respect. Essentially, Don José treated me as a *maestra*, or schoolteacher, because it was a role both he and the community associated most with my research interests. Thus, I was often called maestra or *señorita*, the latter despite the fact that I was a married woman.[10]

Among men, I had to be careful not to give the impression that I was unmarried or otherwise available. With older men, it was much easier for me, because the age difference allowed me to take on the role of granddaughter. For example, I developed close ties with Don Marcelo, the local sacristan. His wife, who had died a few months earlier, had been one of my first contacts because her family had a long history of active involvement in the festival. Almost every day, I found Don Marcelo outside the church or sitting outside his home. I would sit with him and have long conversations about many topics regarding life in Jocotán — its past, its future, the differences he had noticed over the years, living arrangements, the festival, etc. Our discussions were similar to the conversations I had with my own grandfather as he recounted the history of his community as he had experienced it.

With the younger men, however, I had more difficulty, because if they hadn't met me, they tended to make flirtatious remarks, as they would to other single young women. Therefore, I took the precaution of taking one or two children with me whenever I had to interview young men. Since learning about the festival required spending a lot of time among the men, the presence of children signaled that my interest in young men was strictly platonic. I chose to dress very casually (jeans, no makeup, tennis shoes), both for my personal comfort as well as to avoid having people think I was calling attention to myself (i.e., trying to get a man). This is not to say that the young men were not sincerely interested in providing me with important data, only that I had to exercise more caution around young males to avoid any misinterpretation within the community.

In fact, I did establish good rapport with younger men, too. For example, one informant, a young man about 28 years old, came from a family who had participated in the festival for many generations. In addition to performing as a Tastoan, he occasionally performed as a drummer, particularly in the Tastoanes festivals in other, neighboring communities. His father continued to play the role of one of the reyes and his 12-year-old son had recently begun to participate for short periods as a Tastoan. Because of his deep involvement in the festival, he offered a lot of valuable information concerning the festival and introduced me to many individuals who could provide interesting insights as well. Moreover, he accompanied me to another Tastoanes festival in the town of Santa Anita and again served as a sort of guide and contact with members of that community. It was through this man that I came to realize that the Tastoanes participants in the neighboring communities did in fact develop close ties with one another, even though they also developed long-standing rivalries. I also learned that each community celebrated the festival in a unique form and style. For instance, in the neighboring town of San Juan de Ocotán, La Fiesta de los Tastoanes is celebrated in July rather than September and the role of Santiago is assigned according to a ladder-rank cargo system. In contrast, Santa Anita celebrates its festival at the same time as Jocotán, but the celebration lasts nine days rather than three. The biggest difference lies in the acting out of the drama. In Santa Anita, the performance seems far more subdued (though some might say more orderly), in that only one Tastoan can attack Santiago at any given moment. After a three- to five-minute fight, Santiago's helpers put the Tastoan back in line and another Tastoan steps forward to engage Santiago in another bout. From the spectator's point of view, the festival in Santa Anita appears far less exciting and thus draws fewer observers than the other two festivals.

Had it not been for Antonio's involvement in these other festivals, and his willingness to work with me, I would not have had the opportunity to learn about these specific differences in the Tastoanes celebrations. Nonetheless, I had to constantly reinforce the notion that I was a serious person doing important work (again, this is why the role of teacher was most fitting for a young woman). Most people had difficulty remembering or believing that I was married, especially since I had no children at the time and since no one had ever seen my husband in all the years they had known me.[11] Moreover, they thought it strange that my husband, also of Mexican descent, would "permit" me to go alone to Jocotán. Obviously, these concerns were expressed because I was female. Had I been a man, my marital status, my spouse's reaction to my ventures into the field alone, and my lack of children would have been of less interest. Thus, my gender and ethnic status played a significant role in how people responded to me. The constant tension (and sometimes discrepancy) between my own shifting identities led me to seriously consider the ways in which gender is represented in the festival and how these representations relate to the lived experience in daily life, a subject I take up in Chapter 7.

Commentary

In human relationships, the aspects which are most intriguing and complex also tend be those which are most personal and private. Social relationships established in the field are no different. My field experience in Jocotán raised certain concerns regarding my personal background because I shared a similar (though not identical) cultural background with my subjects of study. Gender, age, and ethnicity became key features of my identity, through which the community evaluated my conduct; my occupational status remained secondary. My cultural upbringing equipped me with the necessary knowledge of expected behavior and furthermore, provided an important bond between me and the community that for the most part allowed for a greater degree of intimacy in our interactions. Yet because of this cultural intimacy, I constantly had to be on my guard to avoid breaking social norms even while I was engaging in an activity already outside the parameters of the locally established social categories. That is, as a *mejicana*, I tended to be judged by local standards that would normally not be applied to outsiders. Finally, since many of the Jocoteños were increasingly forced to consider emigrating to the United States as a means of survival, I offered them a glimpse of what their future might hold in terms of my own experiences as a daughter of Mexican immigrant parents and thereby became a resource for them as well.

Living with the particular family that hosted me proved beneficial to my research for two important reasons: first, since they were not strong supporters of the festival, it provided me with a good balance in terms of my perspectives on the role of festival in Jocotán; second, because of the close network among the women in the extended families (i.e., Chela's sisters, mother, nieces, mother-in-law), it gave me an opportunity to deal more closely with women on a more intimate and regular basis. This latter point bears special attention since, as a male-dominated activity, the Tastoanes festival required that I deal more with the men. The intimate sessions with women helped me gain a better appreciation for how the representation of gender in the festival compared to women's perceptions of their actual gender roles.

In general, the field experience provided both my informants and me with a greater insight into our own lives. After my hosts' nine-year-old daughter confronted her father about his need to be more supportive of her mother, I became aware of one way that change could occur. In light of this exchange, and as I reflect on my own encounters with my male host, I now understand those stressful conversations as his attempt to exert some control over me and to establish himself as a powerful male in my presence. Since I was privy to the "behind-the-scenes" interactions within the household, the man worked hard (even to the point of exaggeration) to maintain his public image as a domineering figure. That is, given that the women in his household were intelligent, assertive, and capable, I believe that his probing questions and awkward conversations were intended to both make me believe he controlled his home and abate his own insecurities. But toward the end of my stay, during a family dinner party in honor of his birthday, my male host announced that was he quite lucky to have such a hardworking wife, and that he would work to be a better partner. True to his word, he joined Alcoholics Anonymous to overcome his drinking problem and he began working with children as a religious instructor. By no means did he change completely or immediately, but that he sincerely made efforts to change was a tribute to his wife and daughter, and in more general terms, indicative of the undercurrents working toward developing more equal sex roles.

In terms of my perspective, I tended to be sympathetic with many of the ongoing struggles in Jocotán and I became more sensitive to the complexities the Jocoteños encountered in working to make a living on a day-to-day basis as well as planning for the future. I could understand the frustrations of dealing with a bureaucratic system that made little effort to cover, let alone remedy, its exploitative practices. And after running errands in the hot, smoggy, crowded city of Guadalajara, I could really appreciate the peaceful pace and friendly atmosphere of Jocotán. But, in fact, these perceptions of the living conditions were based upon socioeconomic distinctions. If one could afford to own a car and live in a fancy district of Guadalajara, life in the city could look beautiful, exciting, and safe. On the other hand, living in the city slums was not an alternative Jocoteños were eager to undertake. Thus, I gained a sense of why maintaining Jocotán as an independent community was so important to its residents and why it was so difficult to reach a consensus concerning the best way to do so. I also recognized that their fears of being further absorbed by the city of Guadalajara were not unfounded. And most importantly, I came to understand how the Tastoanes festival, by articulating central concerns within the community, plays a central role in their lives.

Finally, my field experience also provided an opportunity to address another problem common to ethnographers that also bears heavily upon my understanding of this festival.[12] Formerly, anthropologists tended to reduce a community to a single homogeneous group with a single vision, and, in some respects, my work suffers from this tendency. While common sense and experience in the field suggest that such a narrow representation is as unfair as it is unreal, it is nonetheless impossible to report all points of view discovered in the field. Thus, ethnographic writing remains a constant challenge to adequately represent the "others."

THREE

Contested Histories

↓

The most well-known version of the encounter between the Spaniards and the indigenous people of Mexico is the Spanish "conquest" narrative. Most historical accounts advance the view that the Spaniards came and civilized the "primitive" Mexican Indians, introducing them to Christianity and the Spanish language, and providing them with the "benefits" of European ways and customs. For instance, one historian introduces his book, entitled *New Spain: The Birth of Modern Mexico*, as follows:

> The Spaniards conquered Mexico and their adjoining lands because their techniques were superior, their intellect more adaptable and their whole society more flexible than its Mexican–Indian counterpart, which for all its elaborate brilliance and remarkable cultural achievements was still rooted in the Stone Age. (Cheetham 1974, 12)

Such views of the conquest have long been prevalent in Mexican school textbooks. In her assessment of textbooks used in the Mexican public schools in the 1920s, Vaughan claims:

> The nature of race prejudice in the texts was subtle but clear in the treatment of the Indian past. The child would have learned that the pre-Columbian peoples had attained "some degree of civilization" but not a degree comparable with that of the European conqueror. Absorption into the conqueror's civilization was the inexorable outcome of progress. (1982, 218–19)

Even as late as 1975, Friedlander documents various ways in which textbooks fostered a paternalistic attitude towards Mexican Indians, who are portrayed as socially inferior, backward, and uncivilized (1975, 147–52).

Moving from a national perspective to a regional perspective presents both a challenge and an opportunity because the written historical record for most provincial communities remains incomplete. Consequently, reconstructing the historical record for a small community requires a careful study of all available resources written and oral. Collectively, the official documents of the Spanish government, and the early writings of Spanish conquistadors, clergymen, and travelers in Mexico contain more detailed information about the nature of the encounter between the Spaniards and the indigenous people than that available in standard historical texts. But even with access to Spanish historical documents, the record remains tenuous, for given the context of domination, the historical records reflect the cultural, religious, and political positions of the writers. As Donald Brand points out, early historical sources must be used cautiously since they are often sketchy and speculative, particularly in regard to the pre-Conquest and early contact periods (1971, 634–35).

Under these circumstances, La Fiesta de los Tastoanes becomes particularly important for offering a more localized understanding of the conquest, as well as a different perspective concerning the encounter between the Spaniards and the indigenous people. Drawing on a variety of historical resources, I present an "invasion" narrative, which I believe more closely approximates the view articulated in La Fiesta de los Tastoanes, and which claims that the difficult economic and political circumstances under which Jocoteños live today have a long evolution, dating back to the initial Spanish confrontation. Before the arrival of the Spanish conquistadores, the indigenous ancestors of the Jocoteños had managed to live fairly peacefully with their neighboring communities, who shared similar lifestyles and values. As a result of the Spanish conquest, however, radical changes disrupted their religious, political, economic, and cultural lifestyles.

Preconquest Period

Jocotán (Xocotán),[1] an indigenous term meaning "place of bitter fruit," lies in the heart of the Atemajác Valley in the western Mexican state of Jalisco. Before Spanish domination, the area encompassed by the present state of Jalisco constituted only part of the Chimalhuacán territory.[2] Other current states which made up this territory include Colima, Nayarit, and parts of

Aguascalientes and Zacatecas. The Chimalhuacán territory was divided into geopolitical units consisting of groups of townships or settlements. In charge of each unit was a tlatoani, a gender-neutral term meaning chief, leader, or spokesperson in Nahuatl (Topete Bordes 1944, 103).[3] Consequently, these units came to be referred to as tlatoanazgos (or, sometimes, señoríos) by the Spaniards. The exact number of tlatoanazgos remains uncertain because some tlatoanazgos incorporated smaller tlatoanazgos, while others remained independent, regardless of their size (Topete Bordes 1944, 140–41). However, most sources agree that before the Spanish invasion, Jocotán belonged to the tlatoanazgo of Tlalan in the greater tlatoanazgo of Tonallan (Topete Bordes 1944, 123, 125; Navarrete 1872, 7, 10). It is clear that this was not a highly centralized political structure:

La verdad es que no fue ni una cosa ni otra: ni unidad estatal, ni una confederación. Fue simplemente una región poblada de señoríos afines, los cuales, en determinadas circunstancias, principalmente de orden bélico, se conglomeraban y daban la impresión de una federación de pequeños países. (Topete Bordes 1944, 101)

(It was neither a state nor a confederation—it was simply a region populated by neighboring settlements, who under certain circumstances, especially those of warlike character, would unite, giving the impression of a federation of small nations. Under warlike conditions it was the tlatoanis who served as the leaders of the people of the Chimalhuacán territory.)[4]

Within this territory many different languages were spoken, a reflection of the waves of migrants of different tribes, including Teules, Tecuexes, and Caxcanes, who made their way into the region, particularly during the twelfth century (Topete Bordes 1944, 105, 107). Frequent contact and communication among these peoples throughout several centuries, including the peaceful sharing and enjoyment of the geographical environment, led to an intensification of common traits, particularly of beliefs and values. With time, Nahuatl became the lingua franca among these tribes (Ramírez Flores 1980, 82).

In general terms, the Chimalhuacanos shared a similar cultural pattern. They lived in settled villages typically comprised of kinship groups. Houses were either one-room grass mud huts *jacales* or larger adobe dwellings surrounded by lush plants and trees (Topete Bordes 1944, 180). Rather than set in rigid patterns, these houses were scattered throughout the village.

Outside each village, subsistence farming was practiced on communal land holdings. With the aid of simple stone and wood tools, the Chimalhuacanos cultivated corn, beans, chile, sweet potatoes, magueys, peanuts, and cacao. Irrigation improved the land, but a well-organized system of communal labor made agriculture a productive endeavor (Parry 1948, 58). Beasts of burden were unknown before the Conquest, but animals such as the *guajolote* (turkey) and the *teochichi* (a type of edible canine) provided dietary supplements.

Another aspect of culture of central importance for Chimalhuacanos was religion. Significantly, indigenous religion featured male, female, and androgynous symbols.[5] Different gods and goddesses were worshipped within the various regions of the territory. For example, in Tonalá, reverence was paid to Tonatiuh, the sun god, while in the region of Xalisco, the principal deity was Teopizintli, the child god (Topete Bordes 1944, 161–62). In spite of regional variances, Topete Bordes (1944, 165) and Navarrete (1872, 12) claim that, in general terms, the Chimalhuacanos believed in the existence of one invisible supreme being above numerous deities of a second order.[6] These lesser deities controlled the forces of the world, such as the rain, wind, and sun that were vital to the daily existence of the indigenous people. Consequently, it was to these deities that Chimalhuacanos would appeal in times of need.

Religious activities became important communal events not confined to indoor worship, but held, rather, in open spaces where large numbers of people could assemble. Large religious festivals, lasting several days, marked such important dates as the beginning of a new harvest season. Since elaborate festivals were considered especially pleasing to the deities, celebrations were held both to honor them and as a way of obtaining their goodwill and favors.

Music and dance figured prominently in these ceremonies. Although practiced in secular social functions as well, dance was primarily used to communicate with the gods. Music accompanied both forms of dance, and was produced on such instruments as molded clay whistles, bone or carved flutes, and wooden slit drums (Stevenson 1952, 12–13; Topete Bordes 1944, 177). These festivals, further characterized by colorful processions and extravagant banquets, became one of the greatest community enterprises, involving everyone and often attracting visitors from neighboring villages. (As communal expressive phenomena, these celebrations anticipate my present-day concern with La Fiesta de los Tastoanes.)

In sum, the inhabitants of the Chimalhuacán territory developed a lifestyle that allowed for diversity among the various groups. The tlatoani system of political management helped foster a sense of unity among neighboring indigenous communities and proved especially useful for combating invaders who threatened their way of life. For the Chimalhuacanos, the arrival of the Spanish conquerors produced a sense of impending doom.

The Arrival of the Spaniards

The arrival of Don Nuño de Guzmán into Tonalá marked the first direct confrontation between the Spaniards and the natives of this region (Tello 1891, 81–83; Lopez Portillo y Weber 1935, 196–98; Diaz 1966, 19–22). In March 1530, almost ten years after the conquest of Tenochtitlán, Don Beltrán Nuño de Guzmán entered the Chimalhuacán territory, accompanied by a well-equipped army consisting of approximately 150 cavalrymen, an equal number of Spanish infantry, and at least 8,000 Indian allies (Lopez Portillo y Weber 1935, 145). The queen of Tonalá, realizing her people did not stand a chance in battle against the invaders, received Don Nuño de Guzmán peacefully, offering him her lands and people (Tello 1891, 81–83; Lopez Portillo y Weber 1935, 196–98; Diaz 1966, 19–22).[7] The neighboring tribes, however, were not so obliging. Not wanting the Spaniards in their territory, nor wishing to be subjected to their rule, the Chimalhuacanos united in an effort to drive out the enemy. The natives warned the Spaniards not to advance any further or they would be killed. Vocal persuasion proving unsuccessful, and equipped with only arrows, clubs, shields, and stones, the Chimalhuacanos battled fiercely against the Spaniards but were defeated (Tello 1891, 84).

Sporadic rebellions continued during the first decade of Spanish rule, intensifying after a massacre of innocent natives by the Spaniards led by Juan de Arce (Mota Padilla 1870, 115). The desire for independence had not died, and plans for obtaining it had been circulating for some time among the various Chimalhuacán tribes. Among their many complaints against Spanish rule, the prohibition of polygamy stood out as the worst type of invasion of their privacy.[8] Consequently, in an attempt to regain control over their lives, the natives conspired to rid themselves of the invaders. The result was the intensification of this period of rebellion and warfare.

One such war, known as La Gran Rebelión Chimalhuacana de 1541, or La Guerra del Mixtón, was the last major uprising in the area (Tello 1891, 395–97; Ramírez Flores 1980, 19). The war lasted approximately one year. Towns were abandoned as the natives fled to El Mixtón, a mountain very difficult to get to, which served as a fortress for the rebels. This presented a real threat to local Spanish rule, and eventually, additional forces consisting

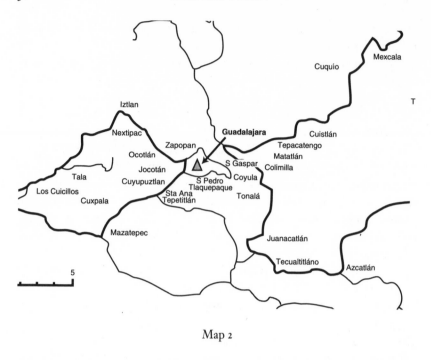

Map 2

of 459 Spanish soldiers and approximately 30,000 Aztec allies were called in from Central Mexico to insure a Spanish victory (Parry 1948, 28). After this war, small independent uprisings occurred occasionally, but they no longer had a significant impact on Spanish rule in the territory. Nevertheless, through other means, such as La Fiesta de los Tastoanes, the memory of these early confrontations with the Spaniards persists.

The importance of La Fiesta de los Tastoanes as a form of documenting and recalling the Spanish invasion is suggested by the fact that this festival has been found in many communities in the Guadalajara region, including Juchipila, Nestipac, Tonalá, San Juan de Ocotán, Mesquitán, San Andrés, Huentitlán, Santa Ana Tepetitlán, and, of course, Jocotán (Map 2). According to Spanish documents, shortly after the first battle in Tonalá, native peoples in surrounding communities immediately began to reenact this battle (Lopez Portillo 1935, 203). Its sudden appearance after the initial battle confirms that dramatic enactments constituted the native form of documenting, recalling, or interpreting important historical events.[9] As such, La Fiesta de los Tastoanes constitutes a critical source presenting indigenous views of the conquest.

The persistence of La Fiesta de los Tastoanes, and the alternative history presented therein, challenges the common perception that the Guadalajara region had little or no significant indigenous population. The lack of large indigenous urban centers in this region has led many scholars to assume that the indigenous population, which they claim was sparse to begin with, declined rapidly due to epidemics and absorption into the general population, so that today no distinctive "Indian" communities survive (Riviere D' Arce 1973; Logan 1984). Certainly the indigenous population and lifestyle was neither as large or as complex as that found in Tenochtitlán at the time of the conquest. Nonetheless, various indigenous settlements existed in and around the area of present-day Guadalajara. Indeed, Gerhard (1982, 132) estimates a minimum of 5,000 inhabitants in the region as a whole at the time of contact, and a 1541 census estimates a population of 2,000 in the town of Jocotán.[10] The question is what happened to these indigenous settlements during the colonial period and after?

Jocotán Under Colonial Rule

During the colonial period, Jocotán continued to maintain some degree of political cohesion and social interaction with its neighboring communities due to the fact that the Spaniards superimposed their system of political rule on the pre-existing forms of local government. Hence, Jocotán, Nestipac, and Santa Ana Tepetitlán became *sujetos* (dependencies) of Ocotlán (known today as San Juan de Ocotán) in the *corregimiento* (district) of Tala.[11] According to the colonial system of rule, at the village level, a native *cacique* (lord, or ruler) appointed by the Spanish authorities and a *cabildo*, or town council, consisting of locally elected officers, managed internal affairs for its township and its sujetos. A Spanish royal officer known as the *corregidor* supervised a district of villages (*corregimiento*), but strict segregation policies prohibited all non-Indians from living in the Indian villages. In this way, native communities became subject to Spanish authority while remaining distinct physical and legal entities.

The segregation strategy constituted a fundamental part of the Spanish system of rule whereby colonial society was divided into two distinct but interdependent nations: a small, ruling Spanish nation comprised primarily of the conquistadors, Spanish bureaucrats, and friars on the one hand, and a subordinate, pan-indigenous nation whose citizens were indiscriminately labeled "indio," thus ignoring existing cultural, linguistic, and political differences among them. The crown established various policies designed to maintain a sharp hierarchical division between the *República de Indios* (Indian Republic) and the *República de Españoles* (Spanish Republic). Legally, indios became wards of the Spanish state, subject to a set of restrictions and obligations.

Under colonial rule, the indios were required to provide tribute (in the form of goods and services) to the Spanish rulers in exchange for legal protection and Christianization. Several methods were developed to extract labor from these indigenous peoples. Under the *encomienda* system, a conquistador was entitled to demand both labor and tribute from the Indians under his charge in exchange for providing them with instruction in the Christian faith and protection of their persons and property (Haring 1974, 40). Since the *encomendero* was primarily concerned with securing a large, steady labor force, he often abused his authority among the natives, exploiting them for their labor almost to the point of enslavement (Parry 1948, 58). As a corrective measure, the crown gradually phased out the encomienda system in favor of the *repartimiento* system. Operating on a rotational basis, the repartimiento drafted a number of Indians from each village to work for Spanish employers for a specific period of time. Although this system provided minimal compensation for services rendered, it nonetheless constituted a system of forced labor.

Both systems of forced labor were used in Jocotán. Up until escheatment in 1594, Jocotán and the other sujetos of Ocotlán were held in encomienda by three different encomenderos. Thereafter, Jocotán provided repartimiento labor throughout the colonial period. Jocotán laborers often worked alongside laborers from neighboring communities in the Guadalajara region (Gonzalez Navarro 1953).

The availability of Indians to provide a variety of services and basic goods was so critical to the existence of the Spanish colonizers that they tended to settle near pre-existing indigenous communities or to create new Indian communities by relocating natives from other areas of Mexico. In the Guadalajara region both situations occurred. Each of the four sites chosen for the city of Guadalajara — Nochistlán, Tonalá, Tlacotlán, and present-day site in the Valley of Atemajác — were selected precisely because they were located in or near pre-existing indigenous communities, which provided labor and produce (Van Young 1981; Riviere D'Arce 1973). The Valley of Atemajác was surrounded by both pre-existing indigenous communities, including Mesquitán, Tlaquepaque, and San Miguel de Mezquitán, as well as the newly founded Indian communities of San Juan de Mexicaltzingo[12] and Analco[13] established by the missionaries.

For a long time, the Guadalajara region maintained a settlement pattern wherein wealthier Spanish residents inhabited the urban center, while the poorer Indian people resided in the outlying communities such as Jocotán,

Nestipac, San Juan de Ocotán, and Santa Anita Tepetitlán (Vasquez 1985, 60). As Guadalajara began to grow in importance and population, it began to physically absorb some of the surrounding Indian pueblos (towns). For example, as early as 1667, Analco and Mexicaltzingo were physically incorporated as barrios of Guadalajara (Riviere D'Arce 1973, 32). By 1800 other neighboring Indian communities, such as Mesquitán, Zapopan, and Tlaquepaque had been physically, if not legally, absorbed (Lindley 1983, 16; Van Young 1981, 26). Because of colonial social and legal policies, however, physical absorption by the city did not necessarily result in the immediate disintegration of Indian communities (Lindley 1983, 16).

A more serious threat to the survival of the Indian communities during the colonial period was the rapid decline of the indigenous population due to wars, excessive work, and epidemics, as well as cultural, psychological, and ecological changes imposed on them by the Spaniards (Aguirre Beltrán 1946, 200). The dramatic decrease of indigenous populations created a severe labor shortage for the Spaniards as well as an opportunity for the confiscation of communal lands. Not surprisingly, one of the most significant outcomes of this period includes the expansion of Spanish land holdings, particularly in the form of *haciendas* (large, landed estates) and in the emergence of a wage labor market (Van Young 1981, 274–75). Nonetheless, as the following report indicates, the native peoples actively strategized to protect indigenous lands:

> *Y aunque con estas enfermedades se han acabado algunos pueblos, no se han despoblado por acá de diez años a esta parte ninguno porque, por conservar las tierras y que no se metan en ellas españoles, en acabándose los de un pueblo envian de otro los vecinos dos o tres indios, y de esta manera hay muchos pueblos con gente como despoblados, y alguno esta vacio y pagan y cuenta en él tributarios y medio, en otros uno.* (Lazaro de Arregui 1980, 89)

(And although these diseases have exterminated some towns, they have not been depopulated for the past ten years because, in order to conserve the lands and to keep the Spaniards out, as the towns diminish in population, those (Indians) from one town send two or three Indians from another town and in this way there are as many towns with people as those without and some are empty and they pay and count tribute and a half, in others just one.)

By the end of the seventeenth century, however, the recovery and growth of the Indian population initiated a competing demand for lands and resources in the region (Van Young 1981). Although the Indians exercised their legal rights wherever possible, the fact remains that the Spanish *hacendados* (hacienda owners) succeeded in taking over the use and ownership of indigenous lands well into the nineteenth century. Without land, the Indians had little choice but to seek employment on the haciendas or move into the urban center as wage laborers. Many a hacienda was large enough to actually sustain an entire community of workers within its boundaries (Van Young 1981; Chevalier 1963). By draining communities of land and people, haciendas contributed further to the disintegration of Indian communities in rural areas. Those Indian communities located close enough to the haciendas to allow workers to commute regularly probably accounted in large part for their survival (Gonzalo Navarro 1953, 14; Van Young 1983, 240). This was especially true in the Guadalajara area, where, for instance, the district of Tala maintained possession of its territory well after the end of the colonial period. Although the pueblos had no communally worked lands, nearly all the land available was fully occupied by Indian farmers (Van Young 1983, 285).

Jocotán Under Mexican Rule

Two important features of Jocoteño history under Mexican rule merit special attention. The first concerns the nature of interactions with the government during the transition from colonial rule to independence. The second focuses on interactions with the modern Mexican government. During the former, the struggle over land rights prevailed as one of the most significant issues, particularly with the rise of haciendas that monopolized land and labor. Throughout the nineteenth century, Indian communities such as Jocotán were subject to a series of practices, legal and illegal, that threatened the very existence of native communities. On the one hand, haciendas weakened the productivity of native towns by depleting them of indigenous labor. On the other hand, haciendas undermined the productive potential of native communities by usurping precious lands whenever and however possible.

The Independence Movement of 1810, which called for the abolishment of slavery and tribute, demanded the restitution of indigenous lands and thus presented a potential resolution to restrict greedy landholders. But implementing social and land reforms entailed complex bureaucratic processes, especially for a new nation struggling to achieve political stability

(Newell G. and Rubio F. 1984, 9). Laws intended to protect Indians and their property rights could easily be circumvented by astute hacendados, who either found loopholes in the legal system to achieve their goals, or changed the existing laws to their advantage.

In Jalisco, for example, the state eliminated the practice of using the terms "naturales" (natives) and "indios" (Indians) in all legal and official documents (Aldana Rendon 1986, 69–70). In this way, liberals sought to eliminate forced tribute payments, especially in the form of labor, but the change in legal status also threatened all special legal concessions made to Indians. Moreover, although the stated intent was to equally divide lands among *los antes llamados indios* (literally, "those formerly designated as Indians," i.e., ex-Indians) of the town, the shift from communal to individual land ownership ultimately facilitated the sale of indigenous lands to outsiders. As Lindley explains,

> Liberals professed to favor breaking up the Indian communities in order to create a yeoman class and make land available for purchase, but they may have had another motive as well. If they could dispossess and uproot the Indians from the land and community, those Indians might form a pool of wage-dependent labor. A landowner or industrialist could then exploit their work without assuming the financial burden of social services usually provided on the great estate (the most important of which may have been extending credit). (Lindley 1983, 108)

The tension and conflict over land continued throughout the nineteenth century. The passing of the 1856 Ley de Desamortización, or Ley Lerdo, once again called for the distribution of communal lands and prohibited corporate land holdings. In addition, new actions targeting indigenous people were also taken. For example, in an effort to minimize indigenous revolts, in 1861 the government passed an ordinance providing for strict punishment for *vagos y ladrones* (vagrants and thieves). Authorities determined who constituted a vagrant or thief, and hence subjected native people to their judgment. Based on this law, in 1862 authorities proposed the legal extinction of Jocotán because of the high number of thieves that inhabited the town.

> *Se propone la destrucción del pueblo de Jocotán por ser el más pernicioso de aquél departamento, a causa de que su vecindario se compone de bandidos y que con su ejemplo fomentan la desmoralización en los niños dispuestos ya a*

todo genero de crimenes. . . . Jocotán ha causado muchos males a los inmediatos
y al los transeuntes en todos tiempos . . . (Colección de Acuerdos 1868, Tomo
III: 184)

(The destruction of the town of Jocotán is hereby proposed for being
among the most evil in the state as this community is made up of ban-
dits who, through their bad example, foster immoral behavior among
children who are exposed to all types of crimes. . . . Jocotán has caused
much harm to locals as well as to travelers in all times . . .)

This decree also mentioned that the community of fifty families living in
scattered huts did not merit the designation of the term *pueblo*, or town, and
it called for the relocation of the families to other towns, where they would
live under the strict supervision of authorities.

The people of Jocotán appealed the decree by agreeing to the following
four conditions: (1) the location of the town would change, reducing it to
one side of the church, and forming linear streets as specified by the town
council; (2) children would attend school every day to ensure good moral
conduct; (3) citizens would chase down criminals in their neighborhood
and guard the highways against thieves; and (4) only people who had established themselves as honorable and well-behaved citizens would be allowed
to reside in the town (Colección de Acuerdos 1868, Tomo III: 429).

This agreement explains, in part, the circumstances under which Jocotán
gradually transferred to its present location alongside the Camino Real, a
major thoroughfare which leads to Guadalajara. The small, thatched-roof
huts were eventually replaced by more permanent dwellings constructed to
accommodate the increasing population. Soon, Jocotán became known as a
posada de arrieros, or resting point for mule drivers. This haphazard and
gradual relocation and reconstruction of Jocotán, ordered by the decree,
explains why it does not strictly adhere to the Spanish grid pattern typical of
most Mexican rural towns. The Catholic church, built in the Franciscan
style popular in the eighteenth century, lies at the edge of town, rather than
in the center. Despite its location, however, the church still functions as the
heart of the town. About half a block from the church sits the small, modest
town hall. The elementary school stands to the right of it, and the churchyard, once a cemetery, now serves as the main plaza where people gather to
socialize (Map 3). Most importantly, however, the memory of that relocation provides a concrete basis for the deep-rooted fear expressed by many
contemporary Jocoteños of being forcibly displaced.

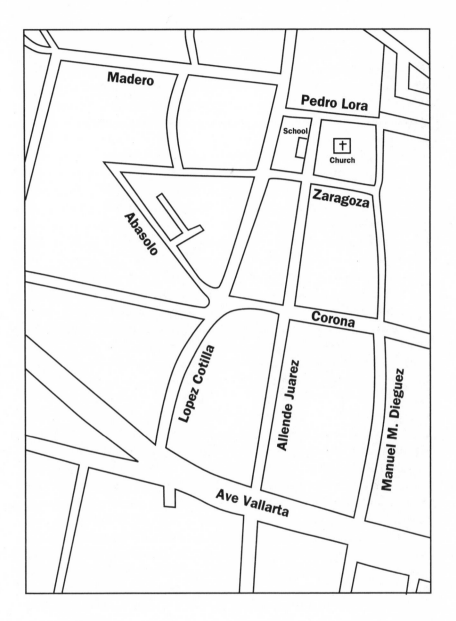

Madero

Pedro Lora

School

Church

Zaragoza

Abasolo

Corona

Lopez Cotilla

Allende Juarez

Manuel M. Dieguez

Ave Vallarta

Map 3

Jocotán in the Twentieth Century

The problems of discrimination and land disputes affecting Jocotán in the nineteenth century reflect the social, political, and economic disparities that plagued Mexican society at large and that ultimately led to the Mexican Revolution of 1910. The Revolution of 1910 attempted to dismantle the repressive, autocratic system that prevailed in late nineteenth-century Mexico. At first the Revolution offered some hope for social change, and indeed, peasants and workers achieved important reforms, especially in the area of agrarian laws that dissolved huge haciendas and reinstated communal lands. But along with these gains, the Revolution brought about major transformations in other domains. After the Revolution, Mexico began to move away from being an agrarian state toward becoming an industrialized, urban community. Together with changes in agricultural production,[14] the growth of industry, which requires wage labor, led to an increase in rural-to-urban migration. However, the rate of absorption of new labor was lower than the overall growth of the labor force, resulting in increased unemployment (Newell G. and Rubio F. 1984, 92). Such conditions forced many Mexicans to seek employment in the United States.[15]

Another important change for Mexico after the Revolution was its rapid increase in population, attributed both to natural reproduction and a decrease in mortality rates (Ryan et al. 1970, 85, 98–99). Coupled with the massive move to the cities, and the limited resources available to a large portion of Mexican society, this population explosion resulted in an increase in the "marginal" population — that is, the unskilled and the unemployable, who have no political voice or clout but who desperately require social services (Newell G. and Rubio F. 1984, 92). Illiteracy, malnourishment, inadequate housing, and underemployment characterize this marginal population.

The Mexican Revolution also brought about the emergence of the *indigenista* movement, an elitist, non-Indian construct prevalent during the post-revolutionary period. A central feature of *indigenismo* was the "optimistic belief that acculturation could proceed in a guided, enlightened fashion, such that the positive aspects of Indian could be preserved, the negative expunged" (Knight 1990, 86). Conceptualizing Indian culture as a disjointed collection of positive and negative practices, indigenistas located obstacles to progress within Indian culture, ignoring external factors which contributed to the marginalization of the Indians. In effect, then, the indigenistas contributed to the tendency to "blame the indio" for their lack of social and economic progress. Commenting on this irony, Knight notes:

Official ideology proclaims their worth, even their superiority (hence
the phenomenon of instrumental indigenismo); but sociopolitical circumstances repeatedly display the reality of prejudice. (1990, 101)

The post-revolutionary changes have effected Jocotán in several ways,
especially because of its location within the second largest cosmopolitan
area in the nation. Offering the best social, cultural, and technological
services in the nation, the Guadalajara region began to attract an ever-
growing number of immigrants after the Revolution, especially from the
rural areas of Jalisco, as well as the neighboring states of Michoacán and
Zacatecas. The massive influx of rural immigrants seeking better educational and employment opportunities, together with an increase in natural
reproduction and a decrease in mortality rates, produced a population explosion in this region that has continued to intensify over time (Walton
1978; Riviere D'Arce 1973). The ever-growing demand for employment,
social services, and housing has become one of the most serious problems of
the century, and there is no easy solution in sight.

Urban expansion in the Guadalajara region has also intensified the struggle for land in Jocotán. To accommodate new businesses and the need for
more housing, the city has repeatedly expanded its borders. Recent reports
reveal that in 1900 Guadalajara had a population of 101,208 and occupied
985 hectares of land, but by 1940 the population had grown to 236,557 on
1,994 hectares, and in 1980 population figures exceeded 225,000,000 inhabitants residing on 22,000 hectares (Vasquez 1985, 57–58). These dramatic growing trends have made land speculation one of the most profitable enterprises in the region (Logan 1984; Walton 1978, 33). Yet they also
present a growing threat to those communities surrounding the city, which
must aggressively defend their territory from investors, opportunists, and
more recently, squatters (Map 4).

New commercially developed residential subdivisions, called *fraccionamientos*, have sprouted up throughout the city and beyond. Sometimes the
plots include commercially fabricated homes, but since these add significantly to each plot's selling price, most working people purchase an empty
lot and construct their own home as the possibilities arise (Logan 1984).
Sometimes government or private industries provide new housing developments for their employees in the outskirts of Guadalajara, where land prices
are relatively cheap. In many cases, *ejido* lands, which are not legally available for sale or rent, nevertheless supply the much-needed space for new
housing projects (Logan 1984, Walton 1978). Illegal or not, "such transactions are routine, if covert, in Guadalajara" (Logan 1984, 29). The constant

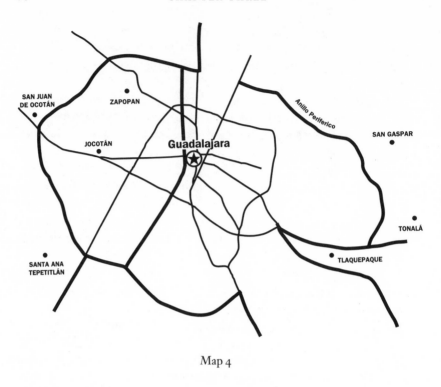

Map 4

development of land around Jocotán unquestionably adds to the locals' fears that one day they may be displaced altogether.

Conclusion

As this brief profile demonstrates, although the political, social, and economic structure within which Jocotán exists has changed significantly since the time of the conquest, Jocotán has nonetheless continued to occupy a position of subordination. During the initial contact period it was quite clear that the new political and economic system was imposed upon the brown, pagan, Mexican natives by the white, Spanish Christians. But as contact intensified, the initial indicators of differentiation became blurred, rendering them obsolete as categories of distinction. Within the religious domain, this blurring, or blending, process is referred to as syncretism (see Chapter 7). Racial typology comprises another notable domain in which this process became evident. The advent of miscegenation rendered the terms blanco and indio obsolete as racial categories, instead making them polar extremes along a continuum of socioeconomic status.[16] By the end of the colonial period, then, the old markers of underlying social, religious, political, and economic factors that, in effect, marginalized Jocoteños were obliterated, but today new ones have taken their place.

Significantly, the annual performance of the festival supports the view that the arrival of the Spaniards marks a memorable watershed in the lives of the indigenous people of the Guadalajara region. The specific moment in history upon which La Fiesta de los Tastoanes focuses is one that forever changed the lives of indigenous Mexicans. Dramatic changes occurred as a result of Spanish invasion and domination. New diseases coupled with destruction of indigenous institutions (even family life, as the Indians knew it, changed) resulted in the drastic decimation of indigenous populations. This is not to suggest that there were no existing tensions among the local natives, that is, the so-called Chimalhuacanos, but rather that the experience of colonization presented a radical break with life as the Indians had known it and united local natives against a common enemy, the Spaniards, and their indigenous allies.

The history recounted in this chapter helps to explain why the notion of invasion and subordination emerged as persistent themes in the lives of the Jocoteños since the Spanish conquest. Because of its geographic location, Jocotán is treated as one of many suburbs that have sprouted up recently around the city of Guadalajara to accommodate the overflow of migrants in search of better employment and educational opportunities. Yet the existence of Jocotán predates that of Guadalajara, and Jocoteños preserve many strong links to their past with respect to identity and cultural practice, loosely referred to as "traditional." As will be shown in the next chapter, features such as reciprocity and networking, respect established on the basis of contributions to the community, faith in supernatural forces, and acceptance of licentiousness as a normal part of life add up to an entirely different world view, one that is tolerant of, but not tolerated by, the linear-oriented, instrumental society that urban Mexico has become.[17] In many respects, the festival reinforces those features of Jocoteño life, thereby revitalizing the Jocoteños' sense of community and their ability to function as a community. Consequently, the festival has become a symbolic representation of a lifestyle that is increasingly threatened.

In Chapters 5 and 7, I will show how the festival narrative not only points up the importance of the initial encounter between the Spaniards and natives in this region, but also articulates the lasting implications of the resulting subjugation of indigenous peoples including the devaluation of their cultural practices.

FOUR

Jocotán Today

⋎

Today, Jocotán can best be described as a paradoxical community. Like other communities throughout the Guadalajara region, Jocotán has increasingly been effected by urbanization — a process which has disrupted and gradually eroded the traditional agricultural-based form of existence. Moreover, like recent suburbs that have sprouted up around large urban centers, its population may be considered largely "marginal." Nonetheless, unlike the newly developed communities, Jocoteños actively maintain cultural and territorial links to their indigenous heritage, and they do so most explicitly through the preservation and performance of the Tastoanes festival.

In this chapter, I explore the relationship between Indian identity and the preservation and performance of La Fiesta de Los Tastoanes, attending more closely to the local meanings ascribed to the term "indio." To this end, I begin by providing an ethnographic description of contemporary Jocotán and then I move to explore linkages between Jocotán and surrounding communities in which the Tastoanes festival continues to be celebrated. By comparing and contrasting these communities with the recently established *colonias* (residential areas) and fraccionamientos around these communities, I hope to illuminate whether and how the festival contributes to the formation of an Indian identity.

The Setting

Jocotán is located on the Guadalajara–Nogales highway approximately 3 kilometers beyond the limits of the *municipio* (municipality) of Guadalajara,

62

minimally a 45-minute bus ride from downtown Guadalajara, depending on which route one takes. Traveling along the Camino Real Boulevard, the stark white church of Jocotán is the first and only visible indication that a community lies behind the facade of factories and cornfields. Otherwise, one can easily bypass the community, as most people tend to do.

The town is situated between two small hills divided by an *arroyo* (stream) which grows to a small river during the rainy season. During periods of intense rainfall, the lack of adequate drainage systems in town pose quite a serious health problem to locals, whose streets become easily flooded. In general, however, the climate in Jocotán is quite agreeable, varying only slightly throughout the year.

Lush trees of various types (eucalyptus, sapodilla, mesquite, oak, pine, and guava) scattered throughout the town provide shade, fragrance, and fruit. Domestic animals such as cows, pigs, burros, and horses — the latter used primarily for transportation and agricultural work — roam the streets, adding to the rural ambiance of Jocotán. Although most of the vacant lots surrounding the town have been bought up and developed, two cornfields lie adjacent to the town and a large vacant field referred to as "la gigantera" serves as a playing field for children.

Perhaps the most striking observation about Jocotán is that despite its proximity to Guadalajara, the material benefits of modernization and technology are not evident in Jocotán. Technically, Jocotán belongs to the municipality of Zapopan, which has sprawled out in an uneven manner over the past twenty years or so due to the large number of displaced rural agrarian workers who are attracted to the city in search of employment. New colonias have sprung up everywhere, including on the agricultural ejido lands. As a result of the rapid and intense rate of population growth in the municipio and the improvisational, and sometimes illegal, nature of the housing developments, the municipal government has provided public services only "in a very inadequate and piecemeal fashion" (Martin 1994, 107). These widespread social and economic conditions of the municipality exacerbate the impoverished living conditions in Jocotán because those new developments only add an additional burden to an already overtaxed system. In this respect, Jocotán is typical of many small, rural communities throughout the state of Jalisco (Riviere d'Arc 1973).[1] Although the new suburbs that have sprouted up around its borders also lack many modern conveniences (Logan 1984; Martin 1994), Jocotán is notably worse off.

Only half of the town has running water. The town has no paved streets or sidewalks. Houses are mostly constructed with adobe brick, although some buildings are covered with layers of painted cement. According to one census figure, approximately 80 percent of the Jocoteños own radios (Noveno Censo de Población 1970, 238). While increasing numbers of families own televisions, the recently established telephone service remains unaffordable for many residents of Jocotán. The postal service is an irregular and limited service at best and, until only recently, Jocoteños generally regarded postal service in their community as non-existent. Thus, as for many other services, Jocoteños must seek full communication facilities in Guadalajara. For day-to-day needs, however, Jocotán boasts twelve small *abarroterías* (general stores), three *mercerías* (dry goods stores), two *tlapalerías* (paint stores), two *tortillerías* (tortilla factories), one *mueblería* (a furniture store), and one *farmacia* (pharmacy). Although the town has no bars, the local pool hall functions as a hangout for men, who ignore the no alcohol signs that are posted throughout and bring their own alcoholic beverages into the establishment.

In this century, the town of Jocotán has experienced a significant increase in population. In 1910, Jocotán reported 387 inhabitants.[2] A slow but steady increase in population began in 1940 with 412 residents, rising to 553 in 1950, and nearly doubling that figure by 1960 with 1,026 inhabitants.[3] By 1970, the population had almost regained its sixteenth-century figure, claiming 1,886 residents.[4] Today, the population is estimated to be above 6,000.[5] The dramatic increase in population may be attributed to a lower death rate as well as to a general increase in urban migration.

Traditionally, very few outsiders have come to live in Jocotán, but this too is changing. Because of its proximity to Guadalajara, and due to the intensification of the recent economic crisis, a growing number of people are attracted to Jocotán, primarily by the lower cost of housing there. For example, one informant told me that she and her family had moved from Guadalajara to Jocotán because it was the only place in which they could afford to rent a house. Nevertheless, housing is scarce and so is the land available for the construction of housing. Ironically, the housing shortage reinforces a traditional value, which is to share limited resources among kin groups. Since properties are passed down from parents to children, the land is gradually parceled out to each child as soon as he or she marries. As a result, it is quite common for extended families to live on one *solar*, or plot, of land. Often, small one- or two-room units are built on each solar for each married son or daughter, but sometimes this luxury is not possible and the families live together in one main house. One problem that results from this informal means of land inheritance is that few people have the actual land deeds to prove ownership.

Aside from providing living space, these arrangements offer the additional advantages that cooperation and the pooling of limited family resources can provide, such as in the lending and borrowing of material goods, services, and money. One obvious and important example is the shared responsibility for daily household chores such as washing, ironing, child rearing, house cleaning, tending to domestic animals (chickens, pigs, rabbits), and preparing meals. Given the limited technological advantages available to Jocoteños (i.e., running water, washers, kitchen sinks, etc.), household chores consume a significant proportion of daily life. Reciprocity is thus an important factor of Jocoteño life, through which residents maximize their resources. Indeed, this fact may explain why families choose to cluster together in close proximity of one another, living next door or across the street from one another whenever possible. But the principle of reciprocity may also carry political implications (see Chapter 6).

Proximity to the rapidly growing city of Guadalajara has also resulted in changes in work patterns. For many generations, Jocotán depended on agriculture for subsistence. As a result of the Agrarian Reform Laws developed after the Revolution, in 1925 the people of Jocotán received 4 hectares of *tierras ejidales* (communal farm lands) for each head of household or single adult at least 18 years of age. Presently, although peanuts, jicama, and other crops are grown, only corn survives as a serious economic activity. However, as a result of national transformations in agriculture, less than half the population depends on farming for subsistence today. Instead, construction-related jobs, particularly in the new developments along the borders of Jocotán, offer a steady but meager income. Additionally, many factories located along Avenida Vallarta employ local residents to fill positions as unskilled laborers. Men predominantly work as *albañiles* (masons, bricklayers), as factory workers, and as *jornaleros* (freelance day laborers), while women, especially those between the ages of 12 and 25, typically work as domestics in Guadalajara or in local factories. The low salaries paid for these services often force workers to assume additional jobs to supplement their income. *Cenadurías*, or informal food stands, set up in the patio or entrance of the family home once or twice a week, have proven to be a popular and profitable enterprise. The sale of *antojitos*, or regional specialty foods, such as pozole, chalupas, or tamales, attract a steady flow of customers and thus provide additional income to families. This practice is also quite common in a variety of towns and barrios throughout the Guadalajara area (Logan 1984).

The shift in employment activities (especially from agriculture to construction) has created serious political divisions among the Jocoteños, par-

ticularly between *ejidatarios* (ejido landholders) and *obreros* (common laborers). In an effort to resolve disputes over political control in Jocotán,
a new colonia was developed in 1965. This colonia, Santa Maria de Jocotán, or *la zona* as the locals refer to it, was established just across Avenida
Vallarta (El Camino Real). Subsequently, the ejidatarios were relocated in
the "zona," and today many of the original Jocoteños occupy this new
development. Now, both Jocotán and Santa Maria de Jocotán each have
their own *delegado municipal*, or local political representative.[6] Despite the
political and geographic division, however, there is a high degree of interaction between these two communities, particularly since they maintain
strong kinship ties.

Education is also limited in Jocotán. The single elementary school is
deficient with respect to equipment, facilities, and services. This presents a
real problem for Jocoteños since quality education represents one of the
few means available for the socioeconomic improvement of their children.
Therefore, anyone wishing to pursue higher and/or better educational
opportunities must seek them within the city of Guadalajara. Since the city
bus system extends its services to the neighboring towns, it is possible
for students (and workers) to commute daily. But the real questions are
whether families can afford to pay tuition at private institutions; whether
students have the required academic record for admission; and whether
they have the necessary *palancas* (personal connections with individuals in
positions of power) to get into the overly populated public schools in Guadalajara. This problem, as well as the others enumerated here, is common
to many lower- to middle-income families in Guadalajara as well, although
they may not always have the expressive resources to articulate their discontent (Martin 1994).

Health-care services in Jocotán exist in the following limited forms: a
general practitioner manages an office in town; a medical student runs a
medical dispensary unit three times a week; and a nurse's aide provides first-
aid, administers injections, and supplies birth control pills. Many of the
health problems in Jocotán can be traced to malnutrition and the unsani-
tary conditions to which Jocoteños are exposed. For example, a recent study
indicts an inadequate sewer system, which results in "rivers of polluted
waters that run through certain parts of the town" as a major health risk.[7] It
bears mentioning that another study cites the lack of potable water, which
leads to gastroenteritis, as the principal cause of death in the state (Riviere
d'Arc 1973). According to the latest census, gastroenteritis is one of the
major health problems, especially among children, in Jocotán.[8]

Professional health care services in Jocotán are augmented by traditional medical practices provided by such specialists as *curanderos* (folk healers), *hierberos* (herb specialists), *parteras* (midwives), and *sovadores* (therapeutic masseurs/masseuses). Curanderos provide treatments considered especially effective for those diseases attributed to black magic spells. In this community, black magical practices are particularly associated with one family, referred to locally as Los Sapos (The Toads) and will be discussed shortly.[9]

Substance abuse is a major problem in Jocotán today. The local nurse claims that at least 90 percent of the deaths among males is alcohol-related. While this figure may be somewhat exaggerated, it does suggest the gravity of the problem. In conversations with married women, the majority identified excessive drinking as one of the major causes of marital problems. Among teenagers, especially males, substance abuse involves the smoking of marijuana and the drinking of alcohol. These vices, however, are found mostly among *pandillas*, or local street gangs, also referred to as *cholos*.[10]

The development of street gangs is a phenomenon usually associated with urban ghetto life. This phenomenon highlights the fact that Jocotán does indeed resemble a poor urban community and for good reason. Guadalajara has grown so rapidly and so extensively that it has all but swallowed up the community of Jocotán. As noted in the previous chapter, the new housing developments constructed along the very borders of Jocotán suggest the real possibility that Jocotán may soon be taken over completely by Guadalajara. Compounding the problem, newcomers are increasingly taking up residence in Jocotán proper.

Given the numerous problems in Jocotán, it is important to note that virtually all the long-time residents claim that they prefer to live in Jocotán than elsewhere. The reasons stated for wanting to live in this community include the following: (1) it's peaceful; (2) it's cleaner and healthier than Guadalajara; (3) there is a lot less traffic; and (4) everyone knows one another. Overall, the general perception of Jocoteños is that life in their community is safer, more intimate, and more relaxed than life in the city or in the newly emerging sites on the outskirts of Guadalajara. This is not to say that Jocoteños are oblivious to the multiple problems in their community, but rather that, from their standpoint, being totally absorbed by the city or moving into a recently established community on the outskirts of Guadalajara would only compound their existing problems. As one ethnographer has noted:

The Guadalajara periphery is not a cultural unity, but a place where segments of families whose backgrounds lie elsewhere and who bring their own customs which are often not shared by neighbors. Such an experience cannot and of course does not breed a sense of community. On the contrary, neighbors are treated with some suspicion. They are unknown quantities, and high crime rate, alcoholism and drug addiction foment a general sense of danger in the environment. This breeds suspicion among neighbors and a general turning inward of families anxious not to enter into problems with each other. (Martin 1994, 115)

The ideal of preserving Jocotán as a separate and "traditional" community is one way that Jocoteños express their resistance to the process of encroachment brought about by urbanization. The key question is how to overcome these problems? Unfortunately, there is no consensus on this issue and the official leaders provide little guidance.

Town Organization

The political factions in Jocotán extend beyond the divisions between the ejidatarios and obreros noted above. Informally, various individuals or groups play some type of leadership role. These include, but are not limited to, the local priest, the DIF committee (*Sistema Nacional para el Desarrollo Integral de la Familia*; i.e., the National System for the Holistic Development of the Family), the Tastoanes mayores, and the old family who practices black magic, referred to collectively as Los Sapos. Each of these groups is recognized as having some power in the community, even if it has no legal or official status, and consequently, their support (or lack of it) affects the quality of life in Jocotán.

As a representative of the state religious order, the priest plays an important role in this predominantly Catholic community. Generally, the priest resides in the community and supervises all formal religious instruction and activities in the town. Formal events include mass every morning at 6 a.m., except Wednesdays, and on Saturday night, Sunday morning, and Sunday night. Additionally, the community holds a rosary every afternoon around 6 p.m. But since the priest strictly dictates what he considers to be the appropriate social and moral conduct in the community, his influence extends beyond the church into the domestic sphere, covering topics such as birth control, premarital sex, substance abuse, and the work ethic. Needless to say, differences around these issues generate tension, guilt, discontent, and sometimes, insubordination, within the community.

Like the priest, the delegado municipal is important as a representative of a larger order, in this instance, the government. As such, his relationship to the community at large is tenuous at best. Appointed by the Presidente Municipal in Zapopan, the delegado controls permits for public dances, secular festivals, and various fund-raising activities. Most Jocoteños I spoke to referred to the delegado as an ineffective community leader interested in the political scene for personal gain. For many, his disrespect for local customs and concerns became most apparent in the communal project to renovate the exterior of the church. The plans called for the installation of cement benches and the planting of trees in the church atrium as a way to enhance the aesthetic appeal (though others suggested the plan was intended to further curb the Tastoanes festival by reducing the space available for its performance). Many locals disapproved of the project altogether, since the atrium had functioned as a cemetery for many years, and thus contained many burial sites. Moreover, family members were obligated to make arrangements to relocate the remains of their loved ones. And the change also meant that, from then on, all newly deceased relatives would have to be buried elsewhere at the family's expense. One old-timer noted that the delegado, like all government officials, had succumbed to corruption, putting personal gain ahead of collective will and well-being. Accused of tricking the community into supporting a project that was not in their best interest, the delegado was viewed as collaborating with outsiders (presumably for financial gain) rather than representing his community. As a result, he reinforces the negative relationship between Jocoteños and the Mexican government.

Los Sapos stand out as another source of negative power. This family openly accepts responsibility for many of the diseases and strange occurrences in town. By claiming responsibility, the family establishes and reinforces its power in the community. Through their alleged powers in black magic, the family has exerted their will on the community. In part, El Sapo's ill feelings toward the community of Jocotán stem from the fact that he claims to have discovered documents proving that he is entitled to certain parcels of land. Unfortunately, this land had been bought and occupied through legal means by other people, who thus have official documents to prove their ownership. Even if El Sapo's documents prove valid, the legal disputes over land ownership could take forever to resolve. Consequently, El Sapo has vowed to get that land back *"por las buenas or por las malas"* ("through good or evil means"). Countless tragedies and ill occurrences have been attributed to El Sapo, who calmly takes the credit within the community, even as he denies any responsibility when questioned by legal authorities. Several informants have stated that *"hasta llora para que lo crean la policía"* ("he even cries so that the police will believe him"). The bottom line is that people do not like him, many fear him, and as is the case with Cyrineo, the character that he plays during the festival, people consider him to be a two-faced hypocrite (see Chapter 7).

The black magical practices attributed to this family merit a full analysis of their own. For the purposes of this study, however, discussion will be limited to the role this family plays in the social dynamics of the community, in general, and the festival, in particular. These points will be pursued throughout the study.

The Tastoanes mayores, or "elder spokespersons or leaders," are well-respected senior men[11] who comprise another important group in Jocotán. As long-time residents of Jocotán, they claim to be descendants of the native Jocoteños and proudly, even defiantly, refer to themselves as "indios." For this reason, they exert significant influence in terms of defending and, to a large extent, defining what is "traditional" in that community. In addition to organizing the Tastoanes festival, they also oversee other community celebrations such as *Los Pastores* (The Shepherds Play), *La Danza de la Conquista* (The Dance of the Conquest), and *La Danza de los Sonajeros* (The Dance of the Rattles). When they become too old to actively participate in the danzas, they continue to act as advisors to the younger generation on matters of indigenous traditions, and they take great pride in promoting and preserving those traditions.

Of the groups identified thus far, the DIF probably offers the most promising avenue for addressing the many problems facing Jocotán. DIF is essentially a federal social program designed to involve marginalized communities in improving their living conditions. Consequently, through participation in the DIF program, Jocotán comes into contact with about fifty of the approximately two hundred distinct communities in the Guadalajara area, some of which are new and others not. Under the supervision of social workers, a committee has been established in Jocotán to carry out special programs and projects. These include a senior citizens' workshop once a week, a children's soccer team, a preschool/daycare center, and a nutrition program in which parents are taught to prepare well-balanced meals for their families. Special projects have been developed in cooperation with various county agencies for delivering or establishing certain services (i.e., postal, telephone, water) in the community.

Although this program is sponsored by the government, its success lies in the structure which requires a solid group from within the community to implement the program. Another distinctive feature of the DIF program is that it is run largely by women. At the national level, Mexico's First Lady assumes responsibility for the program, and this structure is maintained at the state and county levels as well, since the wives of the elected officials also take charge of DIF at their respective levels. In small communities, women may volunteer their services to act as local representatives of DIF. In Jocotán, this has posed a problem at times because some men refuse to work cooperatively with, or worse, subordinate to the women, even though they may share the same goals. For example, the delegado of Jocotán has openly stated that he will not work with *"una bola de viejas"* ("a bunch of hags"). Consequently, it is not easy to achieve the goals set out by DIF members. Indeed, at one of the DIF meetings I attended in Zapopan, the social workers asked the community representatives to air their complaints. Time and again, the women complained that they were able to obtain governmental support for local DIF activities only if they agreed to submit to local authority—something they were not always willing to do.

The Politics of Identity

Danzas, music, stories, and archeological artifacts frequently surface as poignant, if sometimes fragmented, reminders of the pre-Hispanic peoples who originally inhabited this area. On a typical day, music from radios and cassette players fills the air with the locally preferred música norteña, ranchera, and tropicál styles that seem to drown out the cosmopolitan *baladas* (romantic ballads) and American Top-40 pop hits. But sometimes, at nightfall, the eerie sounds of flute and drum permeate the town of Jocotán, as the Sonajeros rehearse their danzas in the church atrium. The trancelike rhythms produced by the dancers' rattles evoke images of ancient nights, of a time when these performances did not have to compete with the blaring electrical sounds, or with the evening soap operas, for that matter. The flute and drum seem to entice community members to step outside their homes and socialize with family, friends, and neighbors. Such occasions often became opportunities for people to reminisce about the past, to ponder the changes experienced within the community over the years. Similarly, each discovery of archeological artifacts by local farmers plowing the fields, or more recently, construction workers building new housing developments, inspires the retelling of a series of "discovery tales." These narratives are always reported as "true stories," even though they are always framed with the disclaimer *"dicen que"* ("they say") as in the following example:

Según dicen que cuando se encuentra una olla llena de ceniza, es un entiero de los antepasados, así acostumbraban ellos. Pero si la olla esta llena de tierra, quiere decir que fue un entierro de dinero pero que se volvió a polvo porque no le tocaba al que lo descubrió.

(They say that if one finds a pot full of ashes, it's the remains of the ancestors, because it was their burial custom. But, if the vase is full of dirt, it means that money was originally in it, but it turned to dust because it was not intended that he profit from this discovery.)

To accentuate the veracity of these stories, people often contribute personal testimonies. For instance, one man declared that one of his cousins had found such a buried artifact and had literally gone mad when he discovered only dirt. (Relatives present at the telling of the story assured me that this cousin is still alive and still crazy!)

This story sparked another treasure tale. This time, the man who uncovered the treasure was allegedly taken ill by the noxious fumes it contained. As a result, he died shortly after the discovery, leaving the money to his brother and a friend. Many locals believed this story to be true because shortly after his death, the man's brother suddenly came into enough money to make improvements on his home and begin a local business. Treasure tales constitute but one type of story which focuses on the strange and unexplained occurrences in town. By far the most common stories of this genre concern the appearance and works of the saints.

Although Santiago represents the most important religious figure in this town, La Virgen de Zapopan and La Virgen de Talpa assume important roles locally as well. Introduced to the area by Fray Antonio de Segovia and Fray Angel de Valencia on December 8, 1541, La Virgen de Zapopan has become one of the most important religious figures in the Guadalajara area (Botello Aceves 1987, 544). Each year, the Virgin travels to each of the communities in the Guadalajara area, where parishioners greet her with a small celebration. But on October 12, *el día de la raza* (the day of the mestizo race), thousands of devotees accompany her on foot as she makes her pilgrimage from the Cathedral in Guadalajara to her home in the Basilica de Zapopan. On the evening of October 11, devotees and danzante groups from the outlying areas, including the Sonajeros group from Jocotán, gather in downtown Guadalajara in the plazas surrounding the cathedral. At midnight, participants begin to walk or dance their way, accompanying the Virgin to her ultimate destination, the Basilica at Zapopan, a ritual which generally is not completed until early the following morning.

La Virgen de Talpa also inspires a pilgrimage in her honor. Locals say that this Virgin was made by a friar out of ephemeral material (corn husk and sugarcane). With time, the Virgin started to deteriorate so the priest asked a cleaning woman, "una indita," to put her away in storage. When the woman went to do so, she noticed that the Virgin had an exceptionally beautiful face that looked almost human. According to legend, the material out of which she was constructed has not faded, despite the many years that have gone by. In fact, they say a mole-like mark on her face was caused by someone who put a cigarette to her face just to see if she would burn. Though she was permanently scarred, she miraculously survived. Such stories contribute to the perception of this Virgin as a powerful deity. People from all over the country participate in the yearly pilgrimage to celebrate her saint's day and to fulfill a manda, or promise made. In Jocotán, even some of the very old women make this pilgrimage, on foot, every year, even though the distance is quite far—at least a four-hour drive by car through the mountains. Now, the pilgrimage is aired on television, they tell me, but they claim that it is not the same to watch the broadcast as it is to participate in the event.

These are just a few of the stories and practices that have been transmitted orally from generation to generation amongst the town folk and that invoke reflection on the past, and ultimately, on the people who lived in the past. But what has become of the indigenous people who inhabited this territory, who once told these stories, who once danced these dances? Have they disappeared through extinction or absorption? And what of the contemporary people who embrace and embody these cultural artifacts as a link to their past? In Jocotán, these are precisely the kinds of sticky questions that people engage in, debate, mull over, and negotiate on a regular basis. Underlying these questions, moreover, is the larger problematic of determining where "Indianness" resides.

Officially, Indians are recognized as part of Mexico's legacy, a part of the nation's past. Despite the fact that the Mexican Revolution advocated pride for the indigenous heritage of the nation, the official rhetoric of mestizaje focused on the Aztecs, Mayas, or other ancient Mexican civilizations in a rather vague and romantic nationalist vein. Implicit in this view is the idea that in modern times the indigenous people have been absorbed into the mestizo nation, except in isolated, rural enclaves, as illustrated in the following statement:

Guadalajara es una ciudad impregnada de civilización y de cultura hispán-icas, los monumentos de estilo colonial que hay en ella son numerosos e impor-

tantes y las tradiciones típicamente criollas han marcado la región, lo cual deja muy poco lugar a los rasgos de civilización indígena. . . . Los pocos indígenas que persisten, refundidos en una montaña de acceso particularmente difícil, son grupos reducidos y en nada introducidos en el circuito cultural o económico de la vida actual de la region. (Riviere D'Arce 1983, 18)

(Guadalajara is a city impregnated by Hispanic civilization and culture, the colonial-style monuments are as numerous as they are important and the typical Creole traditions mark this region, leaving very little room for the [survival of] indigenous features. The few Indians that persist, isolated in an inaccessible mountainous location, are a small group who in no way participates in the cultural and economic life of the region.)

Ironically, despite all the rhetoric to the contrary, the people of Jocotán acknowledge that outsiders refer to them as "indios." As noted in the previous chapter, the term indio was introduced at the time of the Spanish conquest and applied indiscriminately to all native peoples. After independence, the term was no longer used in official documents, but the idea of a distinctive Indian population persisted, as suggested by the awkward label, *"los antes llamados indios."* With the rise of the indigenista movement, the term *indígena* replaced the term indio to refer to people who actively retain a cultural or linguistic connection to their indigenous roots.

By these standards, the people of Jocotán, who speak Spanish as their native language, can only be considered as "Indians" on the basis of cultural practices. Accordingly, when asked, Jocoteños generally define indios on the basis of *tiplecito*, which refers both to the accent and intonation used when speaking (revealing the influence of an indigenous language or dialect), the use of *huaraches* (native sandals), the use of *rebozos* (shawls), and participation in religious fiestas and danzas. Following this logic, an individual could presumably choose to become less Indian by shedding these characteristics. However, upon further questioning, Jocoteños inevitably note that Indians usually lack a formal education, marketable skills, and money, which explains why they occupy the lower end of the socioeconomic ladder. Notwithstanding the criteria of speech and dress, Jocoteños recognize that a resident from the city of Guadalajara would apply the term indio to all residents of Jocotán, since by comparison, Jocoteños are poorer and less educated. In common parlance, the generic term indio has become a pejorative term, often used to connote someone who is uncivilized, backward, and ignorant—qualities that must be erased or overcome in order to ensure cultural progress.

To contest the negative connotations associated with the term indio, some Jocoteños apply this term to themselves, but they do so in a way that runs counter to that propagated through official rhetoric. The people of Jocotán do not claim ancestry to Aztecs, Mayas, or other ancient and well-known Mexican civilizations, as do official discourses of mestizaje. Their claim to indigenous origins is both more humble and more localized, though they reject the notion of indio as naturally or inherently inferior. Instead, when Jocoteños apply the term to themselves, they claim a direct connection to the native inhabitant of this particular area, as oppressed people, dominated by another group, who have nonetheless managed to survive through persistence, compromise, collective effort, and wit. From this perspective the Indian identity is intimately tied to issues of authority and struggles against domination. Jocoteños provide this alternative and much richer articulation of what it means to be Indian through the Tastoanes festival.

In the following chapters, I provide an analysis of the Tastoanes festival and the strategy of hybridization in order to highlight the politics of identity that are embedded in the festival. But it is also important to understand that La Fiesta de los Tastoanes is widely perceived to be an Indian practice despite its hybrid origins. The reasons for this perception are several: first, as noted in the previous chapter, the Tastoanes festival serves as an annual reminder of the indigenous people who inhabited this very area at the time of contact, and provides an alternative account of that encounter. Second, La Fiesta de los Tastoanes thrives in Indian communities. At one time, the Tastoanes festival extended into many Indian communities in and around the Guadalajara zone, including such towns as Tonalá, Mesquitán, San Andrés, and Huentitlán. Today, the Tastoanes festival continues to be celebrated in various communities within the Guadalajara metropolitan zone, including Nestipac, San Juan de Ocotán, and Santa Anita Tepetitlán (see Maps 2 and 4). Significantly, the festival has been retained by the community members with little or no support by church or civil government. In fact, in most towns, the church and local government openly favor the elimination of the festival altogether. Consequently, in choosing to practice and preserve the Tastoanes festival, participants knowingly assume and accept a public, if controversial, Indian identity.

In this sense, the residents of those communities that celebrate the festival seem to appreciate each other as allies in a common cause—the preservation of Indian practices despite all odds. Not only do they attend each other's festivals, they support one another by lending masks and costumes, playing music (chirimía and tambor) and, less commonly, occasionally playing an active role in the festival. Even during non-religious events, members of these communities tend to socialize with each other rather than with those located in closer geographic proximity. For instance, young males from these former Indian communities formed their own soccer league, explaining that they got along better with each other than with residents of the newer developments. Moreover, the fact that the Tastoanes festival is not as widely practiced as it once was is both a source of pride among those who have succeeded in preserving this tradition, as well as a concern over their ability to continue to do so in the future.

But there is also some amount of friction and competition among communities. Conversations concerning who has a better festival, how well it is organized, who is better able to avoid trouble with the police, and who can present a more hospitable image of their community to outsiders reveal a deep sense of always being watched by the general public — a concern about how people will "read" them. Knowing the importance of these dynamics sometimes tempts a few rowdy adolescents to ruin the event for their neighbors. On one occasion, a rock-throwing fight between locals and residents of San Juan de Ocotán threatened to ruin the festival. As people in the atrio scurried for shelter (me right along with them), I heard individuals grumbling *"por eso dicen que somos incivilizados"* ("that's why people say we are uncivilized"). They are always aware of *"lo que dirá la gente"* ("what people will say"). As a result, not everyone in Jocotán is equally invested in claiming an Indian identity.

Nonetheless, by virtue of living in Jocotán, residents are categorically assigned the label of indio, intended usually in the most negative sense, by most outsiders. As outsiders increasingly move within the very borders of Jocotán, the connections between residency and identity will further complicate the social, historical, and cultural claims and definitions of the term. Consequently, members of newly founded communities on the borders of Jocotán make every effort to physically and socially separate themselves from the people of Jocotán.

One incident is particularly telling in this regard. A town plaza constructed on the border between Jocotán and the colonia Pemex, intended for the use of both communities, was taken over by the residents of Pemex, who erected a chain-link fence to keep out the Jocoteños. Claiming that the Jocoteños were *"una bola de indios incivilizados"* ("a bunch of uncivilized Indians") who didn't know how to behave *"como la gente"* ("like people"), the residents of the Pemex community defended their actions. In retaliation, some of the Jocoteño youth proceeded to paint graffiti on the cement walls, an action through which they publicly claimed their right to that plaza. Incidents of this nature reveal the ways in which the politics of identity are played out in daily activities and interactions.

Conclusion

In sum, the politics of identity articulated in Jocotán acquires special significance precisely because the meanings of the term indio are multiple, contested, and the term is employed for different ends. As Guadalajara continues to expand at a phenomenal rate and new communities emerge on the very borders of Jocotán, Jocoteños struggle to maintain their collective identity, their claims to the land, and their folk-religious beliefs and practices. Each of these struggles is intimately linked to the performance and preservation of La Fiesta de Los Tastoanes. Historically, La Fiesta de los Tastoanes has been celebrated exclusively in Indian communities surrounding Guadalajara. Although the communities are no longer legally recognized as Indian in any official sense, the presence of the Tastoanes festival symbolically marks these communities as Indian — a mark that is a mixed blessing, depending on the context. In the dispute over land rights, La Fiesta de los Tastoanes may prove useful as a means of identifying the contemporary practitioners as descendants of the pre-Hispanic inhabitants of the area, especially where no written documents exist to prove ownership. Given the social stigma attached to Indian identity, however, some residents, like many mestizos, choose to disassociate themselves from their indigenous heritage. This is particularly evident among some of the newcomers who reside on the fringes of Jocotán and who treat the Jocoteños and their cultural practices with disdain. No doubt such acts of discrimination have contributed to the gradual disappearance of the Tastoanes festival in many neighboring communities.

On the other hand, Jocoteños would argue that, as mejicanos, "*todos somos indios,*" that is, "we are all Indians." In claiming an indio identity for themselves (and for other mestizos), Jocoteños seek to counter and ultimately expose the anti-Indian sentiments embedded in the dominant ideology of mestizaje, for they do not engage in discourse of racial or cultural "purity" — Indian or Spanish. Instead, Jocoteños openly acknowledge La Fiesta de los Tastoanes, as well as themselves, as a hybrid product. As I demonstrate in the following chapters, through La Fiesta de los Tastoanes,

Jocoteños emphasize that the major opposition between the Jocoteños and "others" (non-indios) has to do with differences in power, privilege, and strategies for survival rather than a list of superficial cultural traits. Hence, the festival serves as testimony to the persistence of the natives in light of oppressive forces and directs attention to the ongoing struggles in which many Jocoteños continue to engage on a daily basis.

A view of the priest smoking as he watches the Tastoanes perform

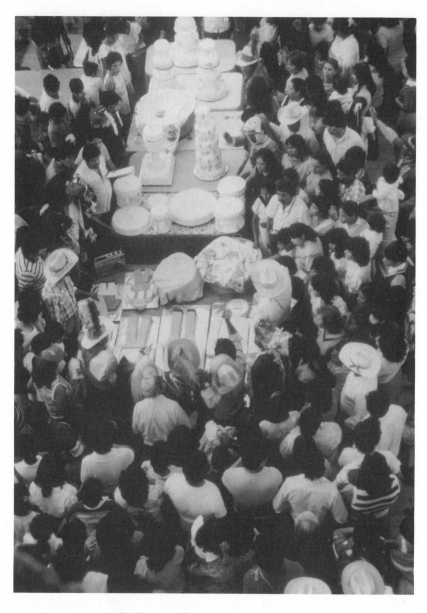

A bird's eye of the collection of the prendas

The Tastoanes mayores as they discuss responsibilities
and obligations of the prenda volunteers

The Tastoanes and several Moros pose for a photograph

The chirimía and tambor players

The final procession ends in the church atrium.

The statue of Santiago as he appears on a daily basis in the church

Cyrineo

The boys show the sticks and milk-carton masks they use for playing Tastoanes

A Tastoan succeeds in making Jacob buck Santiago

Close-up of a teenager's Tastoan mask

The sacristan uses the tiny sword from Santiago's statue
to strike the faithful as a form of penance

Cyrineo tries to revive Santiago by brushing his body with a branch

Santiago prepares to attack a Tastoan
(note how the Tastoan holds his sword to block the expected blow)

FIVE

A Religious Conversion Story

✦

Of the many narratives concerning the encounter between the Spaniards and the natives of Mexico that are embedded in La Fiesta de los Tastoanes, the most widespread and simplistic rendition is that offered by the casual observers who venture out for an hour or two to catch a glimpse of this "exotic" event, or by outsiders who read about the festival in the newspaper. Contemplating the festival for the first time, these observers often ask this: why do the Jocoteños celebrate their own defeat by the Spaniards? And, why do Jocoteños honor Santiago, the patron saint of the Spaniards? From their standpoint, the fact that the festival honors Santiago and deals with the victory of Christianity is enough to conclude that the festival is nothing more than the successful implantation of the Spanish moros y cristianos dance–drama. Moreover, its continued celebration in local communities clearly demonstrates (to them, at least) the supremacy of the Spanish Christians, on the one hand, and the naive and submissive character of the native people, on the other. Such assumptions raise fascinating questions, but in this chapter I consider only one: how does Christianity factor into the politics of identity in Jocotán?

Both the ideas and assumptions outlined above find support in some of the earlier scholarship on the Tastoanes festival. For instance, Frederick Starr reported the following in 1902:

Curiously, it is not the commemorative celebration of some event in which the natives were victorious actors, but of one in which they were defeated and humiliated. . . . There can be little doubt that the tastoanes drama took form under the early Spanish influence. It is an example of the way in which the Indian passion for dances and festival was turned to the advantage of the new religion. (1902, 80)

In contrast to these common but rather patronizing interpretations, La Fiesta de los Tastoanes as practiced in Jocotán is based on a local account which offers another perspective. While most accounts diminish and ultimately degrade the significance and continuation of indigenous religious practices, this particular account takes another approach. Construed as a religious conversion story, this account underscores that the acceptance or appropriation of Christianity does not necessarily imply total conversion or submission to colonial forces. Instead, appropriation of the "other" may merely be a strategy that may be put to different ends, including the transformation of symbolic meanings. In what follows, I present this local account to illustrate an alternative and more localized interpretation of La Fiesta de los Tastoanes, one that challenges the view of natives as submissive or naive.

Don José, a Tastoan mayor who is recognized in the community as one who knows most about La Fiesta de los Tastoanes in Jocotán, provides the following account:

Santiago es un apóstol español, el señor lo designó a evangelizar estas tierras. Lo que consiguió es que la gente lo matara. Lo mataron porque él también los mataba y porque creían que venía a robarles sus tierras. Entonces el señor lo resucitó y le dice, "No pues si te mandé a que los evangelizaras no a que los mataras." "Pues si señor así lo mandaría pero pues no pude de otra manera." Entonces el señor dice, "Mira, el caballo Jacob es tu hermano. Quiero que vayan a domar a esa gente pero sin matarlos." Y así de esa manera fue que logró el Santo Santiago con la ayuda de Dios.

(Santiago was an apostle of Spanish origin who was sent by the Lord to Christianize this territory. Instead, he ended up getting killed because he started killing people and they thought he was conspiring to steal their lands. God resurrected Santiago, but he scolded him, saying, "I sent you to Christianize them not to kill them." "Yes, you did Lord, but I couldn't do it any other way." Then the Lord says, "Look, your brother Jacob will be your horse. Together you must go Christianize them but without killing them." So it was with God's help, that Santiago accomplished his mission).[1]

Don José's account makes at least two immediate points. The first significant point is the idea that during the initial encounter God sent Santiago to assist the Spaniards in Christianizing the natives. While the Spanish conquerors and missionaries no doubt encouraged such a view in order to legitimize their presence in the area, Don José's narrative makes a different point. He stresses that Santiago's supernatural intervention, rather than Spanish superiority (military or otherwise), led to the eventual success of the Spanish Christians. By acknowledging a higher authority (i.e., God), Don José's rendition of the encounter also positions Jocoteños as (descendants of) "God's chosen people," with a right to practice Catholicism. In so doing, Don José simultaneously argues for an understanding of La Fiesta de los Tastoanes as an appropriate expression of the Indians' religious faith — a major point of contention in present-day Jocotán.

Second, the narrative challenges the notion that introducing Christianity provided a legitimate excuse for bringing violence against the natives, or that this mission gave the Spanish conquistadors a right to take possession of native lands. These points become particularly important, given the Spanish practice of prefacing each encounter with a reading of the *requerimiento,*

> a written document explaining the history of the world from Adam, justifying the authority of the Pope and the Catholic monarchs, and requiring the Indian populations to submit and be converted. (Rowe and Schelling 1991)

The requerimiento ostensibly provided the natives an opportunity to submit peacefully to Spanish domination. Read in Spanish, however, the native peoples could not understand the message. Don José's historical narrative directly challenges the legitimacy of the requerimiento as a pretext for waging war, stealing lands, imposing Christianity, and ultimately, forcing the natives into submission. In effect, Don José's narrative exposes the arbitrary unity between Christianity and Spanish political and cultural domination by questioning the conquerors' right to control, if not manipulate, Christianity in order to achieve their political ends.

In Don José's narrative we note that the invading foreigners threaten the Tastoanes' homeland and lifestyle. As such, the Tastoanes seem justified in protecting themselves and resisting domination and thus emerge as "the good guys." The introduction of Christianity alters, or at least complicates, this initial perception. The Spaniards seek to justify their conquest of the New World by framing it as their religious mission. Therefore, by resisting

Spanish domination, the natives simultaneously resist Christianization. In this scenario, the Tastoanes become losers, whereas the Spanish Christians emerge as winners. However, by accepting Christianity, as the Tastoanes ultimately do (albeit on their own terms), they too can become winners. The problem is how to submit to Christianization without submitting to the Spaniards? Or, stated another way, how to become Christians without rejecting indigenous culture and identity? It is precisely this problematic that La Fiesta de los Tastoanes addresses. La Fiesta de los Tastoanes, as celebrated in Jocotán, provides an excellent example of one means through which Jocoteños actively perpetuated their own beliefs by incorporating symbols of Christianity into their indigenous belief system and assigning new meanings to those newly incorporated symbols. In other words, Christian forms were accepted, but they were filled with indigenous concepts. To understand how this is possible, let us examine the historical context in which the Catholic and indigenous religious practices merged.

At the time of the conquest, two important social and religious movements occurred in Spain.[2] First, the *Reconquista*, literally the Reconquest, refers to a series of campaigns to drive out the Muslims (Moors) who had occupied the Iberian Peninsula since the early eighth century. The Reconquista strengthened the link between church and state (Marzal 1993, 144) and also gave rise to the development of the moros y cristianos dance-drama, which celebrates the Spanish Christian victory.

Second, the Spanish Inquisition, an intense crusade against heresy, sought to cleanse Catholicism of pagan influences, as well as drive out the Jews (Ricard 1966, 35). Even Jews and Muslims who had officially converted to Catholicism were considered a threat and thus were subjected to severe treatment, including public interrogations, expulsion, torture, and even death (Marzal 1993, 144–45). Hence, in the New World, the missionaries initially encouraged a complete rupture with native religious practices and presented Christianity as something new and different.

However, the missionaries did not have complete and total control over the indigenous people. As with all other indigenous groups in New Spain, converting the Chimalhuacanos to Christianity posed many problems for the early missionaries. These included language barriers, unreceptive and hostile audiences, the centrality of indigenous religions in the everyday life of the people, and a hugely disproportionate ratio of Indians to priests. Many times, indigenous deities were found hidden behind Christian statues or buried beneath the holy cross (Brenner 1929, 142–44). Unable to enforce a complete rupture with indigenous religion, the friars developed a new strategy. This time, they seemed to have understood the need for color and pageantry which had to be satisfied in any substitution of a new religion for an old. They sought not to destroy these needs and patterns but adapt, utilize, and emulate them. (Ravicz 1970, 31)

The expressive forms inherent in indigenous religions provided the necessary framework for the assimilation of new elements introduced by the Spaniards. The missionaries and conquerors alike substituted Christian saints and images for indigenous gods and idols. Christian churches, in replacing indigenous centers of worship, were designed to allow for open-air religious celebrations. Whenever possible, indigenous religious festivals were moved to Christian feast days to encourage participation of the masses, especially those natives who had not yet adopted the Christian faith. In some cases, the Christian celebrations coincided with seasonal changes, which were observed by the indigenous people in the form of festivals. To insure that all festivals were Christian and not indigenous events, the friars strictly forbade the presence or practice of any indigenous elements, a rule which proved difficult to enforce (Ricard 1966, 264–82).

In part, the difficulty lay in defining exactly what constituted pagan elements. Since dramatic dances, processions, singing, and other forms of festival behavior figured prominently in the cultural and religious traditions of both the Spaniards and the Mexican natives, these expressive forms were allowed to continue, so long as they expressed a Christian theme. Dramas and spectacles were particularly important for communicating Christian concepts since the friars were not fluent in all the native languages and diverse dialects.

It should be emphasized that the practice of allowing or tolerating indigenous elements in Christian celebrations was not always sanctioned by the religious authorities. Instead, these methods proved useful to missionaries left to their own devices, and by 1560, the Catholic religion had replaced indigenous faiths wherever missionaries had penetrated in the New World. But in the process, Catholicism had itself been partially transformed, due to the efforts to adapt it to native practices (Warman 1972, 91). Explaining the process of religious syncretism and transformation in other areas of Mexico, Klor de Alva asserts that, by the seventeenth century,

Christianity had been thoroughly "Nahuatized" by the Indians who considered themselves genuine Christians even as they worshipped many spiritual beings, disregarded the significance of the teachings on salvations and continued to make this-worldly ends the legitimate objects of their religious devotion. (Klor de Alva 1993, 174)

The notion that the appropriation of symbols may occur in the form of a superficial acceptance of them is also substantiated by scholars working in other parts of the world. For instance, speaking of black Africans, Comaroff and Comaroff have noted:

And yet, even as they are encompassed by the European capitalist system — consumed, ironically as they consume its goods and texts — these 'natives' of other worlds often seek to seize its symbols to question their authority and integrity, and to reconstruct them in their own defiance; sometimes through strikingly imaginative acts of cultural subversion and representation; sometimes in silent, sullen resistance. (1991, xii)

Similarly, James Scott points out that peasant societies tend to maintain institutions that are distinct from those developed or appropriated by, and operating within, official culture.[3] In regard to religion, Scott cautions:

Even when peasants nominally adopt and practice the faith of urban elites, they are likely to transform its meaning and practice in ways which are more in tune with indigenous belief. That elites may formally share the same faith must therefore not blind us to the dramatically different meanings that the faith may have for each group. (1977, 283)

Thus, as Scott warns above, the merging of the Christian and indigenous elements in Mexico does not necessarily mean that the natives had totally given up their indigenous beliefs and values. After all, by accepting Christianity on their own terms, they could and did continue their native practices in many instances (Brenner 1929, 135–56; Ricard 1966, 269–78).

From this perspective, La Fiesta de los Tastoanes can be understood as one means through which Jocoteños actively retain beliefs and practices drawn from the "residual culture" inherited from their ancestors. While many of these traditions no longer find a place within the dominant culture, they have nevertheless been maintained by the Jocoteños alongside the imposed traditions through a process of incorporation or hybridization. As Williams notes, these elements of residual culture offer alternatives to the established hegemony. A close examination of the meaning behind certain religious symbols reveals they can and do take on new meanings for the people who employ them.

It is precisely this idea, that successful divinities should be adopted in place of obviously weak ones, that provided the reason for the natives' acceptance of Christian "gods" and Christian rites during the first phase of Spanish proselytization (Klor de Alva 1993, 178).

This point is best exemplified by examining the role of Santiago, which, in Sherri Ortner's term, amply qualifies as a "summarizing key symbol" for La Fiesta de los Tastoanes (Ortner 1973, 1338).[4] By tracing the meaning of Santiago as a symbol from an historical perspective, and then examining that symbol within a specific festival context, I demonstrate that two important transformations in the meaning of the Santiago symbol have occurred: first, the transformation from Santiago as disciple to Santiago as Spanish Christian warrior/leader within the Spanish context, and second, the transformation from Santiago as Spanish warrior/leader to Santiago as physical and spiritual healer within the Jocoteño context. I demonstrate how this new meaning is made explicit in the context of the festival and in the daily lives of the Jocoteños.

Santiago in Spanish Folk History

Much controversy has emerged among scholars over the question of Santiago's alleged evangelizing visit to the Iberian Peninsula.[5] Despite evidence to the contrary, Spanish popular tradition maintains that Santiago not only preached in Spain, but that he was eventually laid to rest there as well. Spanish tradition further claims the Virgin Mary appeared before Santiago, requesting that he build a temple for her in what is now Spain (Starkie 1965, 15). After complying with her request, Santiago returned to Jerusalem, only to be killed with a sword, circa A.D. 44, by order of King Herod Agrippa, who initiated a persecution against the Christians (Stone 1927, 51). According to popular legend, his body was then rescued and miraculously transferred to Spain in just seven days by two of his apostles, who erected a small chapel over his tomb in Compostela in northwestern Spain (Kendrick 1960, 18). For centuries, Santiago's tomb remained undiscovered. Early in the ninth century, however, his tomb was allegedly discovered, causing a great sensation among the Spaniards (Kendrick 1960, 18). Shortly thereafter, new legends about Santiago as a fearless warrior were circulated. Starkie provides us with the following example:

The first great miracle performed by St. James after his long sleep of eight hundred years took place during the reign of Ramiro I in 845 at that legendary Battle of Clavijo. . . . In the first engagement near Albelda, the Christians were defeated and took refuge on Mount Clavijo, and on the eve of the battle the Apostle appeared in a dream to King Ramiro and promised him victory. The next morning trusting the work of the saint, the king attacked with all his forces and suddenly, they saw the Apostle descend from the sky mounted on a white charger, having in one hand a snow-white banner on which was displayed a blood red cross, and in the other a flashing sword. Terrible slaughter ensued and, according to tradition, St. James single-handedly slew sixty thousand Moors and the remnant were routed with appalling losses. (1965, 23)

This image of Santiago as a courageous and invincible horseman captured the imagination of the Spanish crusaders and subsequently became an important symbol for the Spanish conquerors in the New World. Santiago's spiritual and miraculous physical support was reconsidered the decisive elements which determined the success of the Spaniards in their numerous battles against the Moors and other non-Christians. Stories of his miraculous appearance at crucial points in battles circulated in abundance, resulting in rich legends about Santiago.[6]

Thus, celebrations honoring Santiago commemorated the successful end to the more than 700-year struggle to drive out the Moors at the close of the fifteenth century. The Spaniards expressed and reenacted their victory in the dance–drama called los moros y cristianos. Although numerous versions exist,[7] the moros y cristianos dance–drama may be succinctly summarized as follows:

Stripped of all adventitious elements, the morismas are built about a very simple theme, essentially a mock combat, with dialogue, supposed to represent a battle between Moors and Christians, who are divided into two groups of opposing dancers. St. James is almost always the leader of the Christians, and Pilate generally the leader of the Moors. It regularly ends with the victory of the Christians and the triumph of the cross. (Ricard 1966, 185)

Arturo Warman (1972), a Mexican anthropologist who has done extensive research on los moros y cristianos, claims that this dance summed up many popular manifestations found in the Spanish culture of the sixteenth century. Featuring Santiago as a victorious warrior promoting Christianity, the

Moors and Christians dance–drama represented a political, religious, and cultural ideal for the Spaniards. Associated with war, victory, conquest, and great power, los moros y cristianos became an important instrument in the religious and political conquest of new territories, including Mexico. The notion of selective tradition expressed by Raymond Williams (1977) elucidates the motivations for choosing the Moors and Christians dance as part of the religious, political, and cultural conquest of Mexico. According to Williams, the hegemonic process may involve a selectivity of tradition:

> From a whole possible area of past and present, in a particular culture, certain meanings and practices are selected for emphasis and certain other meanings and practices are neglected or excluded. Yet, within a particular hegemony, and as one of its decisive processes, this selection is presented and usually successfully passed off as the tradition, 'the significant past.' What then has to be said about any tradition is that it is in this sense an aspect of contemporary social and cultural organization, in the interest of the dominance of a specific class. It is a version of the past which is intended to connect with and ratify the present. (1977, 115–16)

Thus, as Warman has suggested, the Spanish "selected" the Moors and Christians dance, in general, and Santiago, in particular, as part of their "significant past" because the dance symbolized Spanish cultural and religious ideals: horsemanship (chivalry), the validation of using military forces to promote Christianity, and the signification of power and unity of a people against a common external enemy (1972, 23). In other words, because Santiago had been used successfully in unifying the Spaniards in war and achieving victory, the same symbol was employed when they went out to conquer new territory.

But how are these Spanish cultural and religious ideals communicated in the Santiago symbol specifically? The account provided by Starkie (above) describes Santiago as riding a white charger, carrying a snow-white banner displaying a blood-red cross, and carrying a flashing sword. It is evident that these signs are important means for reinforcing the idea of Santiago as a Christian warrior. Obviously, the cross symbolizes Christianity in general, but it also brings to mind the idea of the Crusade.[8] The white charger indexes the concept of cavalry, while the color white is symbolic of purity, honesty, and goodness. Finally, the sword, which was the weapon used to kill Santiago, becomes, in the Spanish–Christian context, an icon of a weapon to combat any threat to Christianity. Together, the cross, the sword, and the white horse help create the image of Santiago as a powerful warrior fighting for a "just cause." It is no wonder that the Spanish conquistadors created this symbol of self-affirmation and employed it in their political and spiritual conquest of the New World (Warman 1972).

The Appropriation of Santiago as Folk Hero

During the conquest of what came to be known as Spanish America, historian Valle reports, the apostle Santiago allegedly appeared at least fourteen times, helping the Spaniards succeed in their battles against the natives (1946, 19–42). In the region surrounding Guadalajara, Santiago supposedly appeared in three major battles between the Spanish conquerors and the indigenous Mexicans (Tello 1891, 84, 237, 465). According to Tello, Santiago first appeared in the Guadalajara region in a battle which took place shortly after Don Nuño de Guzmán arrived in Tonalá. Santiago reportedly appeared again in 1536, when the indigenous inhabitants attacked the newly founded city of Guadalajara. His third appearance allegedly occurred in the final battle of the Mixtón War of 1541. On each occasion, Santiago appeared miraculously in battle just in time to lead the Spaniards to victory.

Recalling the local legend upon which La Fiesta de los Tastoanes in Jocotán is based, we note that Santiago succeeds in converting the natives to Christianity, after which the Jocoteños become his devoted followers. Historically, it would appear that the Santiago legends in the New World and La Fiesta de los Tastoanes in Jocotán, are simply examples of the hegemonic process, through which Spanish religious and cultural beliefs were transmitted and imposed upon the indigenous populations. However, as Williams reminds us, the hegemonic process is quite complex and is both continually challenged and renewed. Therefore, while the Santiago legends may have been introduced by the Spaniards for the purpose of establishing their dominance in Mexico, they have now taken on a new meaning and purpose in Jocotán. Specifically, Jocoteños have appropriated a Spanish Christian cultural symbol in order to more easily perpetuate their own residual beliefs and practices, which have themselves been transformed over time.[9]

If this is so, two questions must be addressed: How do Jocoteños transform the meaning of the Santiago symbol imposed upon them by the Catholic Spaniards into a symbol for themselves? And, what does Santiago represent or signify to the people of Jocotán? I have already discussed the local history of Santiago (what people believe concerning how and why he came to the area), but now I focus on other activities outside of, but often related to, the festival itself, specifically, the private motivations, expressed verbally and in practice, for honoring Santiago evident in the everyday practices of the Jocoteños, practices which further attest to new meanings assigned to Santiago.

Santiago in the Present

In Jocotán, locals affectionately refer to their saint as El Santo Santiago (literally holy Saint James) and consider him an important spiritual force in their lives. Throughout the year they pray to him for assistance in confronting and solving problems encountered in their daily lives. To request his assistance, Jocoteños frequently place pictures of sick relatives and/or *milagros* (iconic representations of the ailing parts of the body, such as miniature arms, legs, and hearts) on the statue of Santiago, located in the church, so that he will cure them. One woman reports:

Yo tengo mi devoción con él, y casi todo el año no más me pasa algo y "ay santito, ayudame" y ya le rezo, verdad? Le rezo, le prometo su veladora, voy y se la llevo. Para cualquier apuro y todo.

(I am very devoted to him, and almost all year round, when anything happens to me [I say] "Oh, little saint, help me," and I pray to him, right? I pray and I promise him a candle, and I take it to him. For any emergency or anything.)

Numerous stories have developed concerning the many miracles that his followers believe Santiago has performed for them. For example, there is a story about a native of Jocotán who, on the point of being shot by a firing squad during the Revolution, begged Santiago to save his life, in return for which he would sponsor Santiago's festival every year for as long as he lived. The condemned man attributed his salvation to Santiago's intervention and faithfully kept his promise to sponsor the festival. Local stories receive further support and validation with remarks such as *"Ese señor es de aquí, todavía tiene familiares aquí"* ("That man was a local, he still has family here").

Even today, Jocoteños often participate in the festival as a way to express their faith in and gratitude to Santiago. Sometimes participation in the festival is in fulfillment of a manda, or sacred promise, to Santiago. For example, in 1982, the sponsor claimed that Santiago had helped him overcome his drinking problem and he offered the festival in acknowledgment of Santiago's blessing. In 1984, it was widely known that the current sponsor had been gravely ill. Having consulted with various medical specialists — both professional doctors and folk healers — this man turned to Santiago for assistance, in return for which he promised to sponsor the festival.

People also participate in the festival as a sort of insurance against social evils and premature deaths. A young woman named Tina explained her family's participation in the festival with the following story:

Ya, pues, yo estaba embarazada y vino la primera niña y se me murió. Entonces tuve la otra, se me murió. Entonces tuve al niño, el que tengo ahorita más grandecito, y tenía como unos tres meses cuando se me puso malo también de lo mismo. Entonces me dijo mi suegra, "deberías prometerle una manda al Santo Santiago." Entonces el primer año interné al niño el día 10 de septiembre, y los Tastoanes empezaban como ahora, el 8, el 9 y el 10 (de septiembre). Y ése día que se me puso bien malo el niño, era día 10, y me fuí yo a llevarlo al Seguro. Entonces le dejé dicho a mi esposo . . . y cuando vine yo, ya estaba bailando al santito con todo su corazón que le dejara su niño. Pues yo también le prometí vestirlo los 6 años y entrar de rodillas cargándolo.

(Well, now, I was pregnant and the first girl came and she died. Then I had the other [girl] and she died. Then I had the boy, my oldest one now, and when he was about three months old, he got very sick from the same illness. So then my mother-in-law said, "You should make a promise to Santo Santiago." So that first year, I put my son in the hospital on the tenth, and the Tastoanes began like now on the eighth, ninth and tenth. The day he got gravely ill was the tenth, so I took him to the Social Security hospital. I left word with my husband . . . and when I returned, he was already dancing for the saint with all his heart so that he would spare his son. Well, I also promised to dress him [in a Tastoanes costume] and enter [the church] on my knees carrying him [for the final procession]).

Two years later they were blessed with another son, and today both continue to live healthy lives. In gratitude, the entire family continues to participate in the festival.

Stories recounting the miraculous powers of Santiago serve to reinforce the faith people have in this saint and underscore the important role that he plays in their daily lives. They also suggest a tendency toward apotropaism, which Klor de Alva defines as follows:

> Apotropaism is the belief that the very essence of religion is to hold evil at bay; apotropaic rituals are ceremonies that seek to maintain a favorable status quo or to produce one by attempting to propitiate the beyond-the-human forces in the world. . . The religions of the Amerindians before and after the conquest were and are apotropaic. (Klor de Alva 1980, viii)

From this perspective, the religious practices associated with Santiago in Jocotán may be considered "residual" indigenous practices.

Conclusions

When the Spanish conquerors came to Mexico, they imposed an oppositional paradigm which forced the native population to cooperate with them in their conquest, or to become their enemy. This framework did not allow space for natives who wanted to be left alone to pursue life on their own terms. The simultaneous introduction of cultural and religious domination further complicated matters for indigenous people, who had to choose all or nothing. In looking at postconquest history, it is sometimes difficult to identify surviving indigenous practices for two reasons. First, since Spanish practices are better documented than indigenous practices, current Mexican practices are generally attributed to Spanish dissemination rather than to indigenous origins or parallel development. Second, in a conquest situation, the dominant culture will succeed in imposing its beliefs and practices upon the colonized to some extent. But most importantly, the constant negotiation, appropriation, and modification of existing symbols, on the part of both the dominant and the dominated, in a struggle for hegemony leads to a transformation of meanings.[10] Stated another way, social and cultural contexts are crucial factors for understanding, interpreting, and more fundamentally, creating meaning.[11] Established and manipulated by human agents through a process that is fundamentally ideological and political, symbols change in value and meaning over time and space (Weigle 1982). Thus, a mere list of symbols or attributes assumes enduring meanings over time and ignores the intervention of active human agents.

As the discussion on both the daily practices associated with Santiago and the festival practices illustrates, Santiago continues to play a vital role in the lives of the Jocoteños. Although Jocoteños acknowledge Santiago's role as a Spanish–Christian warrior historically, it is his role as spiritual healer and special protector of the Jocoteños that is emphasized in their daily lives and in La Fiesta de los Tastoanes.

Given the precarious social and economic conditions in which Jocoteños must live, the role of Santiago is clearly an important and necessary resource for Jocoteños. This argument is further supported by another festival practice — ritual gifting — which is also considered an appropriate way of honoring Santiago, as well as an indigenous practice. Stressing ideals of cooperation and collectivity, the entrega de prendas ritual links community members to the festival, to each other, and to Santiago. Importantly, it is their belief in Santiago which motivates their participation in this reciprocal gifting system, and it is this aspect of the festival that we explore in Chapter 6.

SIX

The Prenda System

Reciprocity and Resistance

✣

Of all the festival events, the prenda system stands out as a unique, yet obscure and critical, aspect of La Fiesta de los Tastoanes as celebrated in Jocotán and therefore merits special analysis. The *entrega de prendas* (literally, the "handing over" of gifts) ritual constitutes a system of gift exchange through which participants establish a multidimensional network that connects community members to each other and to Santiago in various ways. Ritual gifting in the festival is not limited to the prenda system because all acts of devotion and sacrifice made in honor of Santiago constitute gifts. Personal gifts to Santiago include the various forms of participation discussed in Chapter 1, ranging from playing the role of Santiago in the festival to taking flowers to his statue in the church. Gifting also occurs among community members, particularly in the form of helping fulfill festival responsibilities, whether it be sewing a costume, decorating the church, or preparing and serving food. Nonetheless, of all the gifting practices found in La Fiesta de los Tastoanes, the prenda system best reveals the complex network of interpersonal relationships that are engendered and negotiated through this festival.

The prenda system involves a rather complicated exchange of seven prendas, or special gifts, offered to Santiago (see Table 1). Each prenda has a specific name and consists of food and/or drink as follows:

1. *Corona grande* (the big crown) refers to a cake of at least four layers, similar to a wedding cake.
2. *Corona chica* (the small crown) is a cake similar to the corona grande but smaller in size.

"Entrega de Prendas" System of Exchange

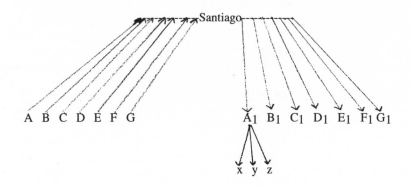

A—Santiago = a dyadic relationship of exchange where A offers a prenda to Santiago in return for his goodwill and favors.

Santiago—A_1 = a dyadic relationship. By accepting a prenda from Santiago A_1 will provide one of equal or better quality at the festival the following year.

A—A_1 = an indirect relationship of exchange (mediated through Santiago) since A_1 actually consumes the prenda offered by A to Santiago.

A_1—x,y,z = a dyadic relationship between A_1 and each person x, y, and z. Next year, x, y, and z will be expected to help A_1 produce a good quality prenda.

KEY: Each letter on the left hand side of the chart stands for one of the seven persons who volunteered to accept a prenda the year before. This year they must give the prendas to Santiago who then divides them among seven new volunteers (A_1, B_1, C_1, etc.). Each new receiver can then further divide his/her prenda with other family members or friends. By doing so these family members or friends will be expected to help that individual reproduce a prenda the following year.

Figure 1

3. *Cuchilla* literally means knife, but the term is used here to mean frame because originally an arrangement of fruits, vegetables, and sweets was placed on a reed frame. In recent years, the cuchilla has been represented by a fancy cake.

4. *Los monos* (the dolls) are large flat sheetcakes in the form of human figures.

5. *El bastimento* (the food supply) is a large basket filled with food and drinks.

6. *La pática* is a local term which in the festival context refers to food such as chicken, rice, and beans.

7. *El desayuno* (the breakfast) consists of sweet bread and hot chocolate.

Each year seven volunteers are selected to receive the seven prendas. Usually, community members interested in being prenda volunteers simply request a prenda from the person playing the role of Santiago. However, since the number of volunteers available almost always exceeds the number needed (seven), priority is given to those individuals who must fulfill a manda and to members of long-established families of Jocotán. For this reason, getting to be a prenda volunteer signals acceptance by the "old timers" or the native Jocoteño community, particularly among the Tastoanes mayores. In any case, the seven individuals who receive a prenda for Santiago one year must provide an offering of the same type and of equal or better quality during the festival the following year. At that time, seven new individuals will receive the prendas.

The prenda system involves several levels and types of exchange, including indirect exchange and dyadic exchange. As Befu points out, indirect exchange involves at least three units, such that A gives to B, B gives to C, and so on, until the last unit gives to A to complete the chain (1977). On the other hand, a dyadic exchange occurs between two parties, and one of those parties may be a supernatural being. The resources that a supernatural being may give include the curing of disease, the bringing of good fortune, and the bestowing of spiritual blessing.

In Jocotán, the prendas are primarily produced and offered to Santiago, both to honor him and as a way of obtaining his good will and favors.[1] Thus, one level of exchange in the prenda system is the dyadic relationship between the giver and Santiago. The givers assume the responsibility of this exchange relationship out of their own free will, often motivated by their desire to express their respect to Santiago, and more frequently, as a means by which to invoke his supernatural power for their own special needs.

At the same time, each gift offered to Santiago is turned over to a new volunteer, who actually consumes the gift and assumes the responsibility of returning the gift the following year. In this way, another dyadic relationship, between Santiago and a new volunteer, is initiated, while simultaneously an indirect relationship between the giver and the actual consumer of the gift is established. In the latter case, indirect exchange operates more as a continuous chain than as a finite cycle among community members. According to Hyde, this type of "circular exchange" allows for little manipulation of the gift by any one individual and therefore promotes positive reciprocity (1983, 16).

There is yet another level of exchange associated with the prenda system. In a private but informal gifting process, the official receiver of a prenda may solicit the friendly cooperation of other individuals for producing a high-quality prenda for the following year by sharing his/her prenda with them. Generally, the person receiving a prenda may distribute the goods that he or she receives among family members or intimate friends and, in this way, hope to secure their support for providing a respectable prenda the following year. The family members or friends usually offer monetary or in-kind contributions for the replacement of the prenda in which they shared. For example, one year a woman receiving the prenda known as los monos, which consists of seven large cakes as described above, explained:

La persona que se lleva una prenda — los monos por ejemplo — pueden dar una parte o un mono a su gente, a sus amistades, o a quien se la pida. Ya para vuelta de año esas personas se las devuelven al encargado o le dan dinero y el encargado las da a los Tastoanes. Así no sale tan pesado.

(The person who receives a prenda — the "monos" for example — can distribute the cakes among family, friends, or anyone who asks. One year later, these six individuals either give a cake or the money [with which to purchase or produce one] to the prenda volunteer, and she turns them in to the Tastoanes. That way it's not such a burden.)

This level of exchange differs from the others in that gifting at this level is optional as well as informal. Individuals may negotiate the terms of this exchange in private and, therefore, reciprocity is not strictly required in the "rules" of the festival. Yet it is socially expected by all participants in this exchange that reciprocity will occur and, therefore, it too may be viewed as a social obligation that must be fulfilled during the festival. At all levels, ritual gifting occurs as a system of "balanced" exchange in which the receiver reciprocates in the equivalent of that received and within a specific time period.

On the afternoon of the second day of the festival, the formal exchange of prendas is mediated by Santiago (that is, by the person who plays that role in the drama), assisted by the Tastoanes who pick up the gifts from the seven individuals' homes. A huge crowd gathers at the churchyard to watch the Tastoanes bring the gifts to Santiago. Santiago carefully reviews his list of gifts received the previous year against the gifts submitted in the current year to ensure that each responsible individual has adequately fulfilled his or her obligation. Judging from the large community turnout for this event, it seems likely that the public display of the prendas acts as a social motivation for maintaining the prendas at a respectable standard of quality. This inference is supported by the way that Jocoteños discuss the size, quality, and general appearance of the prendas and associate the positive or negative characters with those of the giver. If the prenda appears too small, unattractive, or otherwise inferior to that which the volunteer originally received a year ago, Jocoteños will make comments about the stingy and irresponsible character of the giver.

The prenda system exemplifies ceremonial gifting as an effective way of establishing and testing cooperative relationships which are important both in and out of the festival context. People who fail to reciprocate are generally regarded with suspicion and mistrust. Conversely, if one takes his/her prenda obligation seriously, he/she gains in prestige and respect.[2] Most Jocoteños believe everyone should have *"quien responda por uno,"* literally, "people who will respond on one's behalf," or, in more general terms, a support network. Thus, when a prenda is not reciprocated, it suggests that the negligent volunteer was not responsible and that he/she does not have a support network upon which to depend — a further indication that the person cannot be trusted.

One case illustrates the community dynamics. In 1984 the individual playing Cyrineo also took on the responsibility of receiving a prena. Yet, in 1985, he failed to turn in a prenda as required and consequently upset the entire community. During the organizational meeting on August 15, 1986, these community tensions intensified, as this individual proceeded to advise the others on how to behave appropriately during the festival. Filled with indignation, the Tastoanes mayores took him to task for not fulfilling his obligation.

Don Felipe began diplomatically, *"Hay que saber respetar la tradición, si nosotros no hacemos las cosas bien, que será de los demás?"* ("We must abide by tradition, because if we don't do things right, what can we expect from the rest of the community?")

Don Juanito piped in: *"Tiene razón Don Felipe, para eso estamos nosotros, para asegurar que se hagan las cosas como es debido. Hay que ponerles el ejemplo. Además, ésto lo hacemos para el Santito, es cosa seria. Si uno calcula no poder cumplir con las obligaciones pos' pa' que las pide?"* ("Don Felipe is right, that's what we're here for, to make sure things are done properly. We have to set an example. Besides, we do this for the Saint, it's a serious matter. Why take on responsibilities one can't fulfill?")

Gaining confidence by these *indirectas* aimed at Don Chuy, Don Estéban lashed out: *"El año pasado Don Chuy se quedó con la prenda con el pretexto de que estaba enfermo, pues porque no le pidió ayuda a sus hijos, para que se anda comprometiendo si no puede cumplir?"* ("Last year Don Chuy kept the prenda with the excuse that he was ill, well why didn't he ask his sons to help him out, why does he assume responsibilities he can't fulfill?")

To this, others shouted *"es cierto"* ("that's true") or *"tiene razón"* ("he's right"). In his own defense, Don Chuy responded: *"No, no, señores, pues hay que ver que a veces se le complican las cosas a uno, pero no por eso hay que pensar lo peor. Ustedes saben que mi familia siempre ha trabajado en esta fiesta, pos si algo sé, es porque siempre he tomado un interés. Además, no vuelvo a fallar. Es más, pase lo que pase, aunque me enferme o que se yo, mis hijos responden por mi"* ("No, no sirs, you must see that sometimes things get complicated, but you mustn't think the worst. You know that my family has always worked to support this festival. If I know anything, it's because I have always taken an interest. Besides, I won't fail again. What's more, what ever happens, even if I get sick, my sons will cover for me.")

Still disgruntled, Don Jesus asked, *"Ah y por que no respondieron por usted el año pasado?"* ("Aha! Then, why didn't they help you out last year?")

After much heated discussion, Don José intervened to calm the waters: *"Miren, lo que estamos viendo aquí es que tenemos que estar todos de acuerdo. Cada uno tiene que hacerse responsable. Yo desde que abrí los ojos, he sabido que festejamos al santito, es algo muy de nosotros. No hay que dejarla caer. Pues si no hay confianza entre nosotros, en estas cosas sagradas, qué pues? Vamos dándole otra oportunidad a Don Chuy y si nos vuelve a fallar, ya sabemos en que quedamos."* ("Look, what we see here is that we must be in agreement. Each one has to be responsible. Since I first opened my eyes, I have known that we celebrate this festival in honor of the saint, it's something very unique to us. We must not let it end. If we don't trust each other, even in sacred matters, what then? Let's give

Don Chuy another chance and if he lets us down again, we understand the consequences.")

This example demonstrates the seriousness with which the prenda exchange is regarded, and it should be noted that the Cyrineo character continues to be regarded with much suspicion and mistrust by a large portion of the community. Don Chuy is, after all, El Sapo, who allegedly practices black magic. El Sapo is, on the one hand, a self-proclaimed practitioner of black magic who threatens the community, but on the other hand, he is a descendant of one of the oldest Jocoteño families and thus participates in the festival to both assert and cultivate his ties to the traditional sector of the Jocoteño community. As a long-time resident of Jocotán, El Sapo is entitled to participate in the festival, as his ancestors did. But he is also allowed to participate because the community does not trust him and therefore wants to avoid the risk of antagonizing him, for fear that he may cast black magic spells on them. As such, the presence and actions of El Sapo and his family remain constant reminders of the existing tensions within Jocotán.

The above example also emphasizes that participating as a prenda volunteer carries with it the obligation to uphold local traditions out of respect for Santiago, their ancestors, and each other. Through the prenda system social networks are established, linking individuals to each other and to Santiago. The prenda system illustrates that what someone does in the community can and does impact others. But this system works only if everyone understands and honors their end of the bargain. Hence, the prenda system is subject to manipulation as substantiated by the following example.

An aspiring politician told me that although he had lived in Jocotán for about fifteen years, he did not understand why he had not yet been allowed to be a prenda volunteer. Upon further questioning, he explained that serving as a prenda volunteer was important to him because it was "traditional." He hoped to show his support of traditional practices by participating as a prenda volunteer. But failing to articulate any spiritual motives underlying his request undoubtedly made him suspect of using his participation in the prenda exchange system for personal gain. Indeed, it seemed likely that he viewed his potential participation in the prenda system as an opportunity to be viewed as a "local," or "insider," and thus gain the support of the more traditional sector of Jocotán. That the Tastoanes mayores denied his request indicates that they are aware of the potential for people to misrepresent themselves or abuse the system. The moral seems to be that if they have to explain the intricacies and principles of the system to a prospective participant, then the individual is not yet suitable for the post. Participation in the prenda system emphasizes accountability and adhering to the "traditional ways" for ideological reasons, not personal gain. And yet, clearly it is not a foolproof system.

The ties established through the festival assume even greater importance outside the festival context, for Jocoteños rely on these supernatural and social interpersonal support systems for survival in daily life. Through collective efforts, particularly in the form of social reciprocity, Jocoteños meet financial obligations that they otherwise could not afford. The following vignette illustrates the extent to which Jocoteños work together on a daily basis, relying on family members, friends, and el Santo Santiago to survive. *"Unidos se hacen las cosas"* ("United we can accomplish many things"), claimed Tina, responding to my inquires about surviving under one of Mexico's worst economic crises. Tina and her husband both worked hard to make a living, he as a day laborer in construction and she at a local factory. Together, they managed to build a tiny one-room unit on the husband's parent's property, which allowed them to live rent-free. With two sons, however, they had quickly outgrown this home. Tina explained:

> *Mira, el año pasado nuestras familias se pusieron de acuerdo para ayudarnos construir una casita — cada quien con lo que pudiera. Luego, para la fiesta, yo no tenía para comprarle zapatos a mi hijo, y mi suegro dijo, "Ten aquí para que se los compres." Pero así como recibe uno hay que dar también. Cuando operaron a mi papá, yo le rezé mucho al santito para que lo aliviara. Y hasta le hice una manda que por seis años bailaría mi hijo en su fiesta. Y en otra ocasión le ayudamos a mi hermana para que se comprara un carrito, no con mucho, verdad? Pero que se viera la buena voluntad. En fin, ellos también nos ayudan. Por eso digo que unidos se hacen las cosas.*

(Last year, members from both sides of the family got together to help us build a small home. Then, I did not have enough money to buy my son new shoes for festival and my father-in-law said, "Here, go buy him some shoes." But just as you receive, so should you give. For instance, when my father underwent a serious operation, I prayed to Santiago to help my father. I even vowed to have my son dance at the Tastoanes festival for six more years if he cured my father. On another occasion, we contributed money towards the purchase of a car for my sister, not a lot of money, but as a token of our goodwill. After all they help us when they can. That is why I say, united we can accomplish many things.")

Unidos se hacen las cosas expresses a sentiment popular in Jocotán, in which cooperation, strength in numbers, and unity constitute the qualities necessary for success, and even, survival. While numerous examples of cooperation in Jocotán exist, the ongoing internal conflicts described briefly in earlier chapters caution against perceptions of Jocotán as a homogeneous community in which solidarity reigns. Indeed, comments such as *"Somos cuatro y cada quien jala a su esquina"* ("We are four and each one pulls for his/her corner") demonstrate a painful awareness that their already feeble political voice is further weakened by their lack of solidarity. Unity in Jocotán remains an issue of grave concern which requires attention and cultivation. Ritual gifting, such as the prenda system, offers an important means through which Jocoteños may build alliances and foster a sense of community. By associating the practice of social reciprocity and cooperation with religious beliefs concerning Santiago, the prenda system is transformed into a symbolic system that promotes and validates the ideal of mutual assistance among community members beyond the festival context.[3]

The objects of exchange in the prenda system further emphasize the symbolic importance of this form of exchange. The elaborate, and often not very practical, food items that serve as prendas don't lend themselves to accumulation by an individual for personal gain. Instead, prendas circulate strictly as gifts, encouraging further distribution. As such, they underscore the symbolic statement of social cohesion and generosity rather than material gain. Hence, ritual gifting as practiced in Jocotán in the context of La Fiesta de los Tastoanes exemplifies the definition of true gift exchange, or "positive reciprocity," described by Lewis Hyde (1983). To emphasize the spirit of gift-giving rather than the material object of exchange, "a gift must always be used up, consumed, eaten" (Hyde 1983). It is precisely for this reason that Hyde views gift exchange as anticapitalist. He explains as follows:

> Capitalism is the ideology that asks that we remove surplus wealth from circulation and lay it aside to produce more wealth. To move away from capitalism is not to change the form of ownership from the few to the many, but to cease turning so much surplus into capital, that is, to treat most increase as a gift. (Hyde 1983, 37n.)

Mindful of the criticism of overromanticizing gift exchange relationships, I offer Hyde's observations as a way to understand the ideological significance of ritual gifting practices in La Fiesta de los Tastoanes from the Jocoteño point of view.[4] That is, Hyde's view, in my estimation, approximates the perspective embraced by most Jocoteños. Locals generally perceive the prenda system as an indigenous feature of the Tastoanes festival because it is symbolic of the indigenous practice of sharing and cooperation, one they consciously contrast to the "modern" way of life. Explaining why people choose to volunteer for a prenda, Sra. Cásares commented:

> *Porque ésto es cosa indígena, ésto es de generación a generación. . . . Por eso a la gente le interesa como gusto, es gusto decir "Oye, me das una prenda?" Es una forma de contribuir a la fiesta.*

(Because its an indigenous thing, this is from generation to generation. . . . That's why the people are interested, as a pleasure, it's a pleasure to say "Hey, will you give me a prenda?" It's a form of contributing to the festival.)

The perception of social cooperation as an indigenous principle of coexistence stems from their perception of the current, modern capitalist system as one which advocates individualism. Indeed, and this is the second point, Jocoteños contrast their dynamic of mutual assistance to the "every-man-for-himself" mentality prevalent in modern (read capitalist) society which fragments community. Locals know that they have to depend on each other to meet everyday demands. Such demands include obtaining the basics of life — food, healthcare, and childcare. They know that the government is not designed to accommodate their needs. The state offers little in the way of assistance in the day-to-day struggle — no welfare, no free lunch programs, little in the way of medical insurance or services. The government is perceived as a corrupt business, making rich people richer at the expense of poor working people, who remain virtually powerless within the system. To make matters worse, dealing with the bureaucracy causes further frustration and alienation. For instance, when one of Chela's sons died in the operating room, she and her family suspected malpractice. Yet, the doctor was simply "unavailable" whenever they tried to contact him for questioning. As Chela reported, *"Se aprovechan porque saben que no les podemos hacer nada"* ("They take advantage of us because they know we can't do anything to them"). Many more examples could be cited wherein the people view themselves as victims in a corrupt system — yet they have little chance of changing it. All they can do is try to survive by developing safety nets and measures of protection and insurance on their own terms, and, most importantly, to somehow maintain their integrity in the face of human corruption. Thus, for the Jocoteños, ritual gifting in La Fiesta de los Tastoanes has become symbolic of an "indigenous" or "traditional" lifestyle that in certain ways resists the dominant capitalist order.

Working in another part of the world, Nicolas Thomas, captures the crux of my argument well:

> The virtues of gift-giving, reciprocity and egalitarianism in interaction are stressed, not because such practices really (or necessarily) reflect anything that has persisted since former times, but precisely because sharing and parity reverse the rules of the external monetized world, in which such communities are poor and marginal. (1989, 113)

From this perspective, ritual gifting operates as yet another form of residual culture employed by Jocoteños to symbolically critique the capitalist system in which they are virtually rendered powerless.[5] That is, the reciprocal exchange system exemplified in the entrega de prendas represents one indigenous expressive form for dealing with the economic and social uncertainties of life, one which cuts across religious, political, and economic boundaries. Through cultural practices such as ritual gifting, Jocoteños don't simply transform surplus into gifts. Rather, through the exchange of scarce resources a whole economy is created that produces the dynamic of social life. By presenting social reciprocity as the ideal mode of social interaction and exchange, the prenda system also expresses Jocoteños' critique of, or at least discontent with, the larger capitalist system in which they exist.

Conclusion

The discussion of the prenda system explains one way in which festival operates such that several things are accomplished simultaneously. As a dynamic system of festival organization, the prenda system insures tremendous community involvement in the Tastoanes festival; it demonstrates one way in which an individual's role may vary in the festival from one year to the next, thereby providing him or her a different perspective of the festival; it connects the individual and private motivations and practices to the larger social event; it demonstrates the ways in which economic practices are related to religious beliefs; it provides a collective supportive base for festival sponsorship; it reveals information about the nature and quality of an individual's status in the community; and it also exposes community tensions. On the whole, the discussion of the prenda system demonstrates the need to go beyond the "cargo cult" model for understanding the politi-

cal and economic implications of festival participation and draws attention
to festival as a dynamic process.

Through the prenda system social networks are established and reinforced within the festival context which are significant outside the festival
context as well. Reciprocity constitutes an important feature of Jocoteño
life, which is validated in the festival through ritual gifting. Such reciprocity
through gifting also represents an alternative form of dealing with the socioeconomic limitations and devaluations imposed by the dominant order.
Nonetheless, Jocoteños do not exclusively employ an anticapitalist mode of
existence within their community. On the contrary, Jocotán is very much
affected by the current political and economic conditions in Mexico and
participates in the prevailing capitalist economy. Yet, by articulating another kind of economy, however limited, they can express their discontent
regarding their position within the state economy. In short, Jocoteños work
to perpetuate what they perceive as indigenous values and practices, such as
reciprocity, because the Jocoteños can actively participate in them, they
believe in them, and most importantly, they represent a way of life that
works for them.

SEVEN

Compromising Positions

The Politics of Hybridization

✣

The most neutral interpretation of the encounter between the Spanish conquerors and the indigenous Mexicans concerns how the two cultures (and their respective races, religious systems, political systems, etc.) fused together to create a unique mixture. The Mexican state publicly embraces this particular view of the Spanish-indigenous encounter, as evidenced in the inscription at the Plaza de las Tres Culturas in Mexico City which reads, "Neither a defeat nor a victory, but the painful birth of the mestizo people that is Mexico today."

While such statements appear to be impartial, especially when compared to the oppositional paradigm imposed in the colonial period, the fusion between the Spaniards and the indigenous is by no means unproblematic or absolute. Hence, the persistent effort to distinguish between the two and, in particular, to privilege one over the other, continues even today and permeates most aspects of Mexican life, particularly with respect to identity, history, and religion, as noted in other chapters of this book.[1] My specific concern in this chapter is to demonstrate that the Jocoteños and their Tastoanes festival reveal the incessant and sometimes contradictory nature of the process of hybridization.

Hybridization: Incorporating Oppositions

La Fiesta de los Tastoanes represents one manifestation of the Spanish-indigenous hybridization process and takes hybridization as its central strategy.[2] As a hybrid form, the festival encompasses multiple meanings and contradictions. Consequently, La Fiesta de los Tastoanes both allows for resistance to and accommodation of the dominant social order and plays an important role in the ongoing struggle over hegemony.

To illustrate how the strategy of hybridization works in La Fiesta de los Tastoanes, let us return to Burke's notion that collective attitudes towards certain situations are encompassed within a dramatic or symbolic act. According to Burke, the meanings of a creative work (in this instance, the dramatic action in the festival) may be uncovered by identifying the following: (1) the dramatic alignment (what versus what), which involves setting up "equations" that reinforce each of the opposing principles and associational clusters (a list of attributes, images, and acts for each side of the equation), noting the interrelationships that emerge; (2) the situation on which a work opens and closes, paying particular attention to those watershed points or events by which periphery is contrived; (3) the way imagery within the work is linked to life outside the work (1957, 58–60). In what follows, I employ each of these steps to demonstrate the centrality of hybridization in the Tastoanes festival.

Dramatic Alignment

Over a three-day period, the historical narrative of Santiago's first appearance in this area comes alive through a dramatic enactment performed by members of the community.[3] The enactment features vivid representations of the characters and emphasizes certain events within the legend more than others. The Christian Spaniards and the indigenous "heathens" constitute core oppositions, with the differences between the two groups manifested in costume, behavior, and language as described in Chapter 1. Throughout the festival, the differences become further emphasized in both the attitudes and structural organization of each group.

In brief, the associational cluster for the Spanish Christians includes those distinct qualities that characterize them as a group: Spanish culture, their role as conquerors, the Spanish language, Christianity, horsemanship, seriousness, authority, and a strict hierarchical structure.[4] On the other hand, the associational cluster for the Tastoanes group as a whole appears to be quite diverse: male as well as female characters, indigenous as well as Spanish elements, violent as well as nonviolent behavior, a language consisting of Spanish and Nahuatl as well as nonsense words, and human as well as animal figures. In sum, the associational cluster for the Tastoanes suggests a broader, more encompassing system which can incorporate a variety of disparate elements or symbols, including many of those individual qualities characteristic of the Spanish Christians. Compared to the Tastoanes, the associational cluster for the Spanish Christian appears to be very rigid and well-defined, allowing no room to accommodate any new qualities, as the following table indicates.[5]

Note that the opposition constitutes one of inclusion versus exclusion. The Spanish Christian association cluster is a strictly ordered hierarchical category, whereas the indigenous cluster is flexible enough to incorporate complete opposites.

Several theoretical works are useful for interpreting the meaning of the opposing principles articulated in La Fiesta de los Tastoanes. James Peacock's distinction between an instrumental worldview and a classificatory worldview neatly captures the differences between the oppositions articulated in the Tastoanes festival and in Jocotán. Briefly, the instrumental worldview has a more linear conception of history and emphasizes a sequential harnessing of means to an end. It allows no rearrangement or contemplation of symbols, and therefore threatens and is threatened by symbols of reversal (Peacock 1978). The Spanish Christians as portrayed in the drama, with their strict, hierarchical structure, exemplify this worldview well. In contrast, a classificatory worldview "emphasizes the subsuming of symbols within a frame" (Peacock 1978, 223). Since symbolic inversions and reversals call attention to the arbitrariness of the social order by questioning it and providing alternatives to it, the classificatory system allows for critical reflection and can stimulate social change (Peacock 1978; Babcock 1978). The Tastoanes correspond more closely to this worldview.

The opposing principles may also be conceived as embodying the difference between "official culture" and popular or folk culture, as described by the Russian literary critic Mikhail Bakhtin in his influential work *Rabelais and His World* (1965). The fundamental notion advanced in this seminal work is that festival was an integral part of the agrarian lifestyle in pre-class societies in which a multiplicity of voices, views, and approaches to life coexisted. However, the development of class societies led to the establishment of an official culture which promoted one language, one vision of the world, dismissing all others as inferior, invalid, or dangerous. The unilinear official worldview, represented in the Tastoanes festival by the Spanish Christians, essentially prohibits critical dialogue, while the folk or festive approach to life, represented by the Tastoanes, allows for multiple expressions (Bakhtin 1987, 206–58).[6]

Importantly, Bakhtin's work calls attention to the constant tension between the revolutionary (or subversive) and the conservative forces in festival.[7] Lachmann characterizes Bakhtin's contributions as follows:

> This provocative, mirthful inversion of prevailing institutions and their hierarchy as staged in the carnival offers a permanent alternative to official culture — even if it ultimately leaves everything as it was before. It is this irrepressible, unsilenceable energy issuing from the carnival's alternative appeal — and not so much the particular manifestations of folk cultural practice — that disrupts official institutionalized culture. (Lachmann 1988, 125)

Or, returning to Williams's term, the limits of hegemony become more visible through the licentious acts performed by the Tastoanes and the attempt by the Spanish Christians to restrain them. Through their prankish activities and humor, the Tastoanes reveal the oppressive forces that the Spanish Christians represent. Indeed, Bakhtin argues that humor constitutes an important form of communication in festival. Again, Lachmann summarizes this point nicely:

> This inventory or lexicon of symbols contains the schemata for all concretely realized manifestations of laugh rituals: the linking of birth and death, the apotheosis of fools, the humiliation of objects and persons belonging to the official culture, the open demonstration of the concealed (sexuality, digestion), the exchange of socially and sexually specific clothing and gestures, masquerade, the celebration of feasts, the intrusion into the body's or the earth's interior and dismemberment. (Lachmann 1988, 137)

In the Tastoanes festival, we see a striking number of these symbols exemplified: the reyes as transvestites, birth and death of Santiago, humiliation of Santiago and his assistants, and the daily feasts. But it is Bakhtin's discussion of the body that I find most illuminating in analyzing La Fiesta de los Tastoanes, for he claims that the body is the scenario of carnival (1984). The protruding noses and ghastly mouths of the Tastoanes certainly resonate with the grotesque body imagery described by Bakhtin. He also claims that dismemberment, the exteriorization of internal organs, and feasting constitute significant features of festivals. Recall that the Tastoanes take great pleasure in dismembering Santiago's body and feeding his internal organs to the crowd. Here we have a concrete representation of the

Tastoanes consuming and integrating the Spaniards, especially Santiago, into their own collective body. This communion results in the rebirth and renewal of the collective body: transformation through incorporation. Hence, the oppositions represented in La Fiesta de los Tastoanes are ultimately resolved through a process of integration, which is a form of hybridization. Unlike Cyrineo, who has no loyalties and remains a liminal and suspicious character, the Tastoanes work to resolve the oppositions, presenting a resolution to the question of identity, religion, and politics: they incorporate the "other" into their own system, their own being, resulting in a new collective body.

Further evidence of this resolution is revealed by following the next step in Burke's methodology, which involves uncovering the situation on which the festival opens and closes, paying particular attention to those watershed points or events by which periphery is contrived. The festival sequence may thus be summarized as follows: the highlight of the first day occurs around noon and consists of the killing of Santiago. After lunch, Santiago is resurrected, and the jugadas, or skirmishes, between the Tastoanes and Santiago become the main activity of the festival until the final procession. The final procession marks the end of the drama and the beginning of the healing rite. During the procession, the Jocoteños return to their roles as ordinary people, a move marked by the removal of their masks, and Santiago undergoes a transformation in which he is no longer viewed as a violent warrior but rather as a healer of and for the people — specifically the Jocoteños.[8] Santiago's new role is concretely manifested in the use of his sword, which has been changed from a weapon of violence and death to an instrument for spiritually and physically healing people. In the closing ritual, Santiago's sword is no longer used to fight with the people but rather to heal or bless them. Santiago transmits his blessing in two ways. First, people line up before the individual playing the role of Santiago and ask him for several strikes on specific parts of their bodies. In addition to, or instead of, that healing act, they may also undergo the blessing ritual by entering the church, where the sacristan taps community members with the small sword from the Santiago statue. Santiago (the actor) completes the entire ritual transformation by undergoing the sword ritual himself in the church, signaling to the community at large that both the man and Santiago submit to a higher order in seeking justice and well-being.

By emphasizing Santiago's presence and power only after he is resurrected by God, the sequence of the festival highlights Santiago's spiritual power and superiority rather than his role as military leader for the Spaniards. The healing ritual which occurs at the church as Santiago strikes the faithful with his sword highlights the transformation in the role of Santiago from warrior to healer. Further, this healing ritual encompasses the collective body because the healing power, embodied by Santiago, becomes available to everyone. The oppositions introduced in the festival are thus resolved because Santiago is transformed, reclaimed and redefined as a local character who has the power to revitalize and regenerate the community. In this way, the theme of communal regeneration is acted out in La Fiesta de los Tastoanes.

Festival and the Real World

Finally, we must compare the imagery within the festival to the everyday world of the Jocoteños. By examining who participates in the enactments and who takes what role, we can look at the oppositions discussed above to suggest how these relate to the everyday world.

In comparing the Cyrineo role and the individual who plays it, we can see parallels between the festival and daily life that are quite astounding. Earlier in this study, I noted that this role is essentially that of a traitor who has no loyalties. As it turns out, the person who has assumed this role for the past ten years is in fact considered a dangerous and suspicious character in everyday life. I speak here of El Sapo, discussed briefly in the earlier chapters of this study. The reader will recall that El Sapo holds an ambiguous position in Jocotán; he alternates between supporting and threatening the community. Thus, El Sapo, like Cyrineo, is an anomalous character who represents a real danger to Jocoteños.

In contrast, the role of Santiago is generally played by a middle-aged, married man (approximately 35 years old or older). As the principal sponsor of the festival, with an emphasis on his role as provider and defender of the community, Santiago represents the ideal man. Consequently, playing the role of Santiago in the festival becomes a highly desirable means through which males may increase their social status and respectability in the community.

The Tastoanes mayores comprise another category of distinction. Since all of the Tastoanes mayores have previously occupied various roles in the Tastoanes festival, collectively they have become reservoirs of knowledge and experience. Having worked in the festival for most of their lives, these men have proven themselves as respectable and trustworthy individuals who can be counted on to uphold the ancestral traditions. Hence, in everyday life, men who participate as Tastoanes mayores tend to be well respected, senior members of the community.

For young males, festival participation as a Tastoan is one indication that they are entering manhood because it requires strength, skill, and indulging in licentious behavior that is not permissible for little boys. Bauman and Abrahams, in their work on festival (1982), have aptly demonstrated that it is not uncommon for people in the community who tend to be somewhat rowdy and licentious in daily life to assume such roles within a festival context. In such cases, the principle of exaggeration, not inversion, dominates. Indeed, the men who act as Tastoanes tend to be those who enjoy a degree of licentiousness in their ordinary lives, since at their age (traditionally, these are single men at least 15 years of age or older), they have no formally recognized responsibilities in the community and therefore are free to challenge the status quo.

Not surprisingly, women and young children traditionally have not been allowed to participate as Tastoanes, except under special circumstances. Women and young boys may assume roles within the drama, especially if their purpose in doing so is to fulfill a manda. In these cases, they perform as Tastoanes, since there is no limit to the number of Tastoanes who may participate, and generally they will perform for only a brief period of time. For example, they may perform for an hour each day, or they may choose to perform only during the final procession. Infants and toddlers may fulfill a manda by attending the festival dressed up as a Santiago or a Tastoan.

Rarely do parents make young girls responsible for fulfilling a manda through participation in the Tastoanes festival. As girls get older, however, they may choose to participate. Usually, female participation occurs during the teen years, when girls begin questioning or challenging the established norms, or when they themselves make a religious vow. For instance, a 15-year-old girl danced as a Tastoan in 1986 in honor of her deceased brother, who had been a faithful participant until his death. In another case, a teenage girl, encouraged by her male cohorts, participated as a novelty. In that example, her friends stood by her to ensure her safety, since it is well known that in such cases the other male participants will often play rough with the female novice as a way of discouraging her participation. As Maria reports:

> No más una que otra se anima porque es muy peligroso. Hace dos años le quebraron la mano a una muchacha. Se la quebraron al instante y por eso digo que pues, no cualquiera se anima a ponérsela. Tiene que tener mucho valor para ponérsela.

(Only one or two will participate because it's very dangerous. Two years ago, they broke a girl's hand. They broke it instantly, and that is why I say not just anyone will wear it [the mask]. One must have great courage to wear it.)[9]

Teenaged women who participate as a novelty are often identified by the community as *marihuanitas* (marijuana smokers) or cholas because they associate with some of the street youths.

In more general terms, we can compare the oppositions represented by the Spanish Christians and the Tastoanes to the oppositions between the officials (church and government) and locals (indigenous folk culture) in the everyday world. Like the Spanish Christians in the festival, the priest, local government officials, and the police all work to discipline the Jocoteños into the capitalist system, to insure that they are good, productive workers and consumers who remain politically and economically subordinate (see Chapter 3 for details).

The Tastoanes, on the other hand, represent the position of the locals, who resist total and complete subordination by adapting to and incorporating aspects of the imposed official culture. Through the use of exaggeration, inversion, juxtaposition, and humor, festival participants make visible what is usually obscured. As a result, the Tastoanes festival both reenacts and represents an alternative approach to life that threatens and is threatened by contemporary Mexican urban society. Through the festival, the Tastoanes delineate what Jocoteños perceive as the fundamental differences between traditional Jocoteño life and contemporary industrial, capitalist, urban life. Just as the authoritative, hierarchical Spanish Christian group attempts to impose its order on the obstreperous Tastoanes in the festival, so too do local authorities, in particular, and modern urban life, in general, work to restrict the lives of the Jocoteños. In this way, the festival becomes an act of resistance to the current hegemonic order.

Nonetheless, hybridization requires that the Tastoanes in some way conform to the social rules and comply with orders from the authorities to some degree. It is their position within the festival context that most closely parallels the situation of many people of Jocotán who manage to negotiate between "official," or dominant, culture and local, or "indigenous," culture. The licentious behavior of the Tastoanes in the festival context has been subject to more rigid controls in recent years. For example, in years past, the Tastoanes exchanged stolen elements of Santiago's costumes (i.e., hat, sword, spurs, dengue) for items at local stores, thereby forcing Santiago to pay for the goods when he went to retrieve his stolen belongings. Another mischievous act involved taking entire cases of soft drinks or beer off the delivery trucks that dared to enter the town during the festival.[10] Currently, delivery trucks avoid this problem by either making deliveries in the early morning before the festival activities get under way, or canceling deliveries during festival days altogether. And to insure that the Tastoanes abide by the stricter controls, the police from Guadalajara make frequent visits to Jocotán during the festival, at the request of the local priest. While the Tastoanes will not succumb completely to the authorities, they recognize the need to reach certain compromises in order to continue the festival.

However, not all of the contradictions of operating within a polarized framework are easily resolved. Hence, La Fiesta de los Tastoanes both allows for resistance to, and accommodation of, the dominant social order, and plays an important role in the ongoing struggle over hegemony.

Two cases illustrate these points well: they are (1) the conflict between folk and official religious practices, and (2) the conflict between gender roles and relations. The role of the church, particularly through the acts of its local agent, the priest, exemplifies the discrepancies between the locals and the official Catholic church. As a representative of the state religious order, the priest plays an important role in this predominantly Catholic community. The priest in residence between 1980 and 1987 was very adamant about the moral codes people should follow and he expressed great concern about controlling licentious behavior such as drinking and sexual freedom. Thus, he forbade the use of birth control pills, objected to the practice of free unions between men and women, and opposed festivals and social dances, because he believed they promoted sinful behavior. To enforce these moral codes, the priest punished individuals who violated his codes by denying their right to receive communion or attend church. For example, the priest banned one woman from attending church because her daughter had eloped.

In another case, the priest refused to say mass because a dance was being held in a yard directly across the street from the church. Before leaving, he stated that *"las cosas de Dios no se mezclan con las cosas del diablo"* ("the things of God must not be mixed with those of the devil"). The priest's reaction upset almost everyone in Jocotán because they thought he acted rashly and unfairly. In the first place, the number of people attending church that evening was so great that many people were left standing in the courtyard and around the side entrance. While the dance music could be heard in the church, the priest could have chosen to either close the church doors or requested that the music be toned down or stopped altogether until after mass. Instead, he made his statement and walked out on his parishioners.

Parishioners criticized the priest for showing no concern for the numerous devoted people who had come to church rather than, or at least before, going to the dance. As one older woman put it, *"No vamos a los bailes, al único lugar que vamos es a la misa y ahora hasta eso nos quiere quitar"* ("We don't attend dances, the only place we go to is mass and now he even wants to take that away from us").

It is the festival, however, that has represented the biggest point of contention between the priest and the Jocoteños. As the local church authority, the priest's permission was required to use the church, to remove the saint from the church, and his cooperation was needed to officiate four masses. The priest had no intention of participating in, or in any way encouraging the festival. In a private interview (which he did not allow me to record), the former priest of Jocotan arrogantly stated that Jocoteños were *"inditos que no saben otra cosa"* (" 'little' Indians who don't know any better") and they had to be taught the right way to worship.

He thus worked hard to eliminate the festival. His major complaints against the festival included the public drinking, the amounts of money spent on the products consumed during the festival (e.g., food, prendas, flowers, candles, fireworks, etc.), and the general "pagan" nature of the festival (e.g., the processions, the dance–drama, and the drinking). He created many obstacles to its successful performance, such as refusing to hold mass, prohibiting the Jocoteños from using the church atrium for the performance of the drama, and inviting policemen from Guadalajara to patrol the festival.

The priest's opposition to the festival created a great disturbance in Jocotán. His refusal to cooperate resulted in a threat from the local community to run him out of town. Ironically, his fervent objections compelled many locals, even those who were not active participants or supporters of the festival, to openly express support for the festival as a way of expressing their outrage with the priest.

Because their folk-Catholic forms of expression (especially with regard to Santiago) were once acceptable, or at least tolerated, within the official Catholic doctrine, Jocoteños legitimately claimed that their practices fell within those officially sanctioned boundaries. They argued for the validity of their religious beliefs on several related grounds: first, that the Tastoanes festival has been celebrated for as long as anyone could remember and thus the traditional practices had been sanctioned by their ancestors; second, that the Tastoanes festival had received the full support of previous priests; and third, that Catholic practices are not consistent from one community to another. As one woman observed:

Porqué tenemos que abandonar nuestra fiesta que nos dejaron nuestros ante-
pasados? Y porqué a nosotros nos obligan abandonarla cuando otros la siguen
festejando? Y entonces porqué el Padre ——— *nos decía que estas tradiciones*
eran sagradas y que deberíamos conservarlas?

(Why should we give up our festival, which was handed down from our
ancestors, just because this priest says so? If we must abandon our
festival, why do other communities get to keep theirs, and why did
Father ——— [the previous priest] tell us our festival was a sacred
tradition which we should not give up?)

In essence, because folk-Catholic practices vary in time and space, Jocoteños can locate their own beliefs within the broader context, and thus
argue that their local established practices are valid forms of religious expression, and indeed legitimate forms of Catholic expression. Jocoteños
argue that since Santiago was an official Catholic saint, and since he had
traditionally been honored with the Tastoanes festival, it was the priest, not
the Jocoteños, who was breaking with the proper established form of religious expression. In other words, symbolically, Santiago has become a
special medium through which Jocoteños express their version of what
Catholic religion should be. The discrepancies that exist within the official
Catholic religion and the local religious folk-Catholic practices underscore
the fact that while Jocoteños are excluded from any decision-making processes at the official level, they can and will make decisions for themselves at
the local level.

Clearly, then, the Jocoteños do not rely on the priest to mediate their
relationship with El Santo Santiago. One informant summed up his view of
the priest's authority this way:

El padre no más es padre, no es para que venga a mandar aquí. La Fiesta no se
puede quitar de ninguna manera.

(The priest is only a priest, he can't come and rule here. There is no
way that the festival can be abolished.)

Unable to abolish the festival, the priest resorted to attacking it, claiming
that it promoted excessive drinking. Insofar as liquor flows freely throughout the entire festival period, the priest had a point. Although it is the
Tastoanes who indulge most in ritual drinking, alcohol is accessible to most
people who attend the festival. According to the Tastoanes interviewed,

drinking helps them endure the three long days of dancing and fighting in the hot sun. They further defend the benefits of consuming alcohol by pointing out that even Jacob (the horse) is given liquor to fortify his courage and endurance during the festival. (Partaking of intoxicating beverages to increase military potency is an ancient indigenous practice.) However, because alcohol abuse is a major problem in Jocotán, the priest and other critics blame festival participants for allowing, if not endorsing, public intoxication.

In general, Jocoteños do not view liquor per se as evil, and in fact, there are certain occasions and events in which drinking is considered appropriate, if not necessary. Most of these events are social and religious rituals, such as weddings, funerals, baptisms, and, of course, community festivals.[11] Therefore, while most Jocoteños would agree that excessive consumption of alcohol is detrimental to the social and physical well-being of an individual, they would argue that it is also a matter of degree and of context. As one informant stated:

Al padre no le gusta la fiesta porque no es de aquí y no entiende nuestras costumbres. Tomamos para animarnos y aguantar tres dias de danzar con ganas.

(The priest doesn't like our festival because he is not from our community and he just doesn't understand our ways. Drinking is necessary to warm the spirit and to help us endure three days of intense dancing.)

One example clearly highlights the distinction made between ritual drinking and alcoholism in Jocotán. In 1982 a man plagued by alcoholism played the role of Santiago in fulfillment of a manda. He promised Santiago to sponsor the Tastoanes festival if the saint would help him overcome his drinking problem. Commenting on how Santiago had helped this man overcome his disease, various Jocoteños cited this example to illustrate that ritual drinking is not synonymous with alcoholism. Nonetheless, public pressure has led the Tastoanes mayores to curb the amount of drinking that goes on in the festival.

From another perspective, Robert J. Smith, a researcher of religious folk expressions in Latin America, claims that local stories concerning a saint's special powers and goodwill bestowed upon a community "imply that there is an authority (the patron) whose relationship with the people is a direct one, not mediated by officeholders, either religious or secular" (Smith

1975, 73). The notion of maintaining a direct link between the saint and the community helps explain the schism between the Jocoteños and their local priest.

Despite the conflict between Jocoteños and their priest, locals generally tried to maintain a polite neutral position, at least in public. However, when an occasion arose in which the priest insulted the community in my presence, everyone became free to openly criticize him. It was as though once I had witnessed his insults, it was okay for them to let me know how they really felt. Following the incident reported earlier, when the priest left mid-mass claiming that the music from the dance across the street was too loud, Chela disclosed another case in which the priest's nieces were violently attacked, both physically and verbally, by two of El Sapo's daughters. This incident caused a great commotion in town and many, particularly my hostess, saw this as an opportunity to run Los Sapos out of town, or at least to let them know that they couldn't get away with this behavior. Consequently, Chela and her sisters took the nieces to the doctor, who signed a medical report describing the wounds. However, when they brought the document to the priest so that he could press legal charges against the attackers, he simply told them to forget it and announced that he was moving out of town. Frustrated and feeling betrayed and rejected, Chela and her sisters had no choice but to drop the case. But the implications to the locals were clear — the priest simply did not care about the welfare of the Jocoteño community. Moreover, this incident strengthened the power of Los Sapos in Jocotán, who proved once again that they could bully the community. The priest's move away from Jocotán seemed to highlight his disdain for the community, and eventually, to the satisfaction of both parties, a more diplomatic priest took over. Although the new priest does not fully accept all the local practices, and is particularly opposed to the use of alcohol, he seems to be more tolerant of the festival, as indicated by his willingness to officiate masses. His tactic seems to be one of gaining the people's trust by expressing a real interest in their well-being, as well as a respect for their local practices. In this way, he works to modify their practices gradually rather than to demand immediate changes. The approaches of the two priests may be compared to Santiago in Don Jose's narrative: like the eager but violent Santiago, the former priest tried extreme tactics, which resulted in hostility and conflict. The newer priest, like Santiago after God's reprimand, employs gentle measures of persuasion that allow for a long-lasting resolution or compromise.

The discussion of the conflict in religious practices illustrates the "cracks" in the hegemonic system. These cracks in the system allow the community to exert some control over their own lives. With respect to the former priest, the festival can be seen as act of resistance to the hegemonic order.

Conversely, the festival in some ways accommodates the hegemonic order as well, as one final category of oppositions illustrates. Among the most powerful oppositions raised in the festival are those involving sex roles and gender. Peggy Sanday (1981) maintains that the patterns of behavior in a symbolic manifestation, such as festival or religion, are usually consistent with gender roles in everyday life. In her words, "Religious symbols and social form are part of the same underlying blueprint" (Ibid., 216). In his study of Mexican festival, Brandes makes a similar claim:

Invoking religious authority and relying on supernatural favor, fiesta leaders knowingly or unknowingly impose particular conceptions of gender, ethnicity and other types of social relations on the general populace. (1988, 5)

The prominence of males emerges as one of the most salient features of La Fiesta de los Tastoanes. As a cultural script, the drama leaves little room for women: the protagonist is male, the actors are male, and even the sponsor is male (Sanday 1981, 35). However, this public realm obscures some of the most fundamental aspects of the festival, such as ritual gifting, organization, and private worship, all of which involve a more balanced participation along gender lines. Many of these less public, but nonetheless significant, aspects of the festival are rooted in indigenous practice.

The most likely explanation for the schism in gender representation in the festival context is that it reflects the fusion of two distinct cultural practices, that of the Spanish colonizers and that of the indigenous people. Given the context of colonization, the Spanish features had to be the most obvious or immediately evident ones, while the indigenous practices were maintained in discreet and sometimes covert forms. In a similar vein, speaking generally of the Nahua response to Christianity in the sixteenth century, Klor de Alva asserts:

The syncretic integration of new and traditional beliefs and modes of worship did not exclude a certain quite conscious dichotomy between the public sphere where Christian rites predominated and a domestic sphere where change, having come more slowly after the Conquest, was never so great as to make pre-Contact vestiges disappear. . . . The public-Spanish–Christian world did not negate a private-Indian–non-Christian sphere; each complemented the other and each called for what was appropriate under the circumstances. (Klor de Alva 1980, vi)

Hence, in the Tastoanes festival, the public/private division corresponds to Spanish/indigenous practices, respectively. The public realm, in which men figure so prominently, is the dramatic enactment. Here, the domination of the Spaniard over the Indian, the Christian over the pagan, the male over the female, prevails.

By now, the view that there is a direct relationship between male dominance and the cultural disruption brought by Western colonization has been well documented. In her study of Aztec women, for example, Nash (1980) shows how colonization exacerbated the poor treatment of women by decreasing their rights and respect. Similarly, Silverblatt (1981) has eloquently documented the devastating effects of the Spanish conquest on native women's lives in the Andes. Leacock and Nash (1982) and Pike (1990) note the prominence of females in Latin American indigenous religions. As these examples suggest, there is sufficient evidence to conclude that whatever the indigenous gender roles may have been before the Spanish conquest, women's roles worsened, rather than improved, as a result of colonization. The prominence of men in both festival and everyday life suggest that this feature of dominant culture has become, to a large extent, an integral part of local culture as well.

In present-day Jocotán, gender roles implicate powerful contradictions. On the one hand, men often depend on the support and advice of effective community activists, even when they are female. This is so in the festival, where women play supportive but critical roles behind the scenes, and in the household. Similarly, the DIF organization espouses the theory that wives of male politicians should play a supportive role by implementing state-funded social services, such as nutrition programs, recreational activities for children and senior citizens, and health services for the community at large. But the resistance to women as public leaders presents a real barrier for women who have otherwise proven themselves to be good and effective organizers. Public political positions are viewed as "male" domains. Indeed, men will sometimes resort to manipulative tactics to keep women "in their place" by actively undermining any projects headed by a woman that might position her as a viable community leader. Chela candidly noted this as the main reason she appoints males in her family to execute certain tasks.

Por celos no se hacen muchas cosas. A mi lo que me importa es que se hagan las cosas, aunque tenga que poner a mi esposo o hermano por delante.

(Many things don't get accomplished due to jealousy. What matters to me is that they get accomplished, even if it means I have to put my husband or brother in charge.)

In effect, in everyday practice, as in the festival, two conflicting patterns of behavior appear with regard to gender. Sanday explains that in situations where opposing and conflicting sexual power principles coexist, mythical male dominance may emerge as a way station. Coined by Susan Rogers, the phrase "mythical male dominance" refers to

> patterns of public deference toward men as well as their monopoliza-
> tion of positions of authority and prestige. . . . The myth of male
> dominance does not determine ordinary behavior: males do not actu-
> ally dominate, nor do either males or females literally believe men to
> be dominant. . . . The perpetuation of this "myth" is in the interest of
> both peasant women and men because it gives the latter the appear-
> ance of power and control over all sectors of village life while at the
> same time giving to the former actual power over those sectors of life
> in the community which may be controlled by villagers. (1975, 729)

In Jocotán, male dominance is expressed in the festival and in community affairs in terms of male monopolization of public positions of authority or power, as well as in everyday ritualization of male power, such as my en-counter with my male host reported in Chapter 2. In this way, men achieve an image of superiority which obscures the fact that women have more power than is publicly acknowledged. And although the lived reality indi-cates that actual but informal power and leadership have little to do with gender, public roles are reserved almost exclusively for males. By examining the issue of gender, we find that the struggle for hegemony is a dynamic that produces contradictory results. On the one hand, when discussing gender roles, we can see how certain aspects of the dominant culture have been accepted into indigenous culture, both in the everyday realm and in the festival, especially as men struggle to keep women in "their place." On the other hand, as the exchange between father and daughter reported in Chapter 2 and the small but growing number of female Tastoanes indicate, women are working to change gender roles. Consistent with the changes I witnessed in personal interactions, the festival, too, supports the fact that women are increasingly working to expand their roles, and to redefine their male counterparts' roles as well.

Conclusion

Hybridization figures centrally in La Fiesta de los Tastoanes. The process of incorporation does not necessarily imply a smooth and easy union between the Spanish and the indigenous domains. As the discussion of gender roles and relations starkly reveals, hybridization may also be understood as the incessant process of appropriation by both the dominant and the dominated group in the struggle for hegemony, hence, the contradictions and multiple meanings. But this liminal space created through hybridization is a means through which locals have tried to articulate, maintain, and promote ideals they perceive, and indeed claim, as "traditional," ideals that encourage multiple dialogues, contemplation, and critical reflection. This process of adaptation and incorporation, or hybridization, remains critical for Jocoteños. Indeed, the strategy of hybridization is best understood as a process which enables the tolerance of contradictions in order to move beyond the dualistic paradigms so entrenched in Western thought (Anzaldua 1987, 79–80). Through this festival, the Jocoteños articulate their willingness to allow the expression of various ideological voices within their own system, simultaneously express their resistance to the total domination of a linear authoritarian worldview that threatens and is threatened by symbolically rich means of apprehending the world. More importantly, by recognizing themselves and their local customs as the product of two cultures, both indigenous and Spanish Jocoteños—for they do not engage in discourse of racial or cultural "purity"—ultimately expose the anti-Indian mentality embedded in the dominant ideology of mestizaje.

EIGHT

Competing Forms
of Cultural Reproduction

✙

Throughout this study, I have demonstrated that the annual performance of La Fiesta de los Tastoanes generates multiple narratives and perspectives concerning the encounter between the Spaniards and the indigenous people — narratives which often contradict or in some way challenge the official or mainstream accounts. To appreciate the political and ideological importance of these narratives, we must consider them in the context of cultural reproduction, which draws attention to the various forces and contradictions involved in the struggle for hegemony. For it is in this site, the site of primary cultural reproduction, that the struggle for hegemony will be won or lost.[1] For this reason, I am particularly interested in the space occupied by children, where two competing forms of socialization, that controlled by local culture and that controlled by the national or dominant culture, come into conflict.

In this chapter, I show where and how the Mexican state and other dominant forces emerge in Jocotán. As Cockcroft has noted, the repressive forces in Mexico that constitute the dominant culture — the church, media, and the state (which includes education) — are not "necessarily coordinated or unified but together have resulted in a complex powerful bloc of repressive forces" (1983, 278). Echoing Cockcroft's observation, others have commented:

> The political bureaucracy that took shape in the 1960s is also composed of cliques, clusters, and factions; on that basis, these types of political leaders build up their power by commanding factions of politicians, by managing key state-owned industrial concerns, by holding

key government offices, and — foremost — by controlling the source of ideological "power" (i.e., televisions stations, newspapers, textbooks, the party's propaganda offices and the like). Particularly in recent years, this latter power base, the control of ideology, has been key in attaining hegemony. (Newell G. and Rubio F. 1984, 86)

In order to compare the impact of these institutional forces that constitute the dominant culture against forms of local culture, I provide a description of the children's daily activities, since many of these practices bear directly on ideological meanings.

Children are highly visible in Jocotán. They spend most of their time in the community and only leave town under the supervision of a trusted adult, usually a relative. While they can be found watching television, especially soap operas, at almost any time of day, they are usually to be found out playing nearby their homes, in empty fields and lots, or in the churchyard.[2] Sometimes a large group of children, particularly the older school-aged children, will get together to play a formal game such as soccer or hide-and-seek. But regardless of their age, children spend much of their free time outdoors rather than inside their homes or away from the community.

The prominence of children in public spaces in Jocotán has at least two implications. In a recent study, Martin observes that the "streets" may offer children a reprieve from obligations and restrictions imposed on them in the schools and in their homes — a point to which I will return later in this chapter. However, there are other considerations as well. For instance, by spending time in public spaces, children are among the first to see, and be seen by, outsiders such as myself, and they therefore often assume the role of interlocutors and intermediaries between adults and outsiders. Carrying news, filtered with their own opinions, children become important sources of information for their families and help shape opinions of outsiders. From this perspective, the time spent outdoors enables children to keep abreast of local news.

It is difficult to tell how many children actually live in Jocotán since the census reports do not provide this information. According to a recent report, the local elementary school operates on a double-session basis to accommodate a total of 684 students.[3] With the 1986 census reporting a total population of approximately 6,000, the number of students enrolled in school obviously does not correspond to the number of school-aged children in Jocotán. While low enrollment figures may be partially explained by the fact that some students attend school outside of Jocotán, they also confirm that others have dropped out of school altogether.[4]

Although school and play take up a significant part of a child's day, each child must also contribute to the family maintenance in some way.[5] Even during the school term, children are expected to participate in household chores before and after school. For instance, milk and tortillas are generally bought on a daily basis and sometimes before each meal. Other common household chores include running errands for their families, sweeping the streets, washing dishes, helping attend to domestic animals, and taking care of younger siblings.

The relationship between siblings is particularly interesting, for although the age difference may not be more than a year or two, the eldest child usually is given responsibility for the rest of the kids — a task that can begin as early as age 3 or 4. Older children treat their younger siblings with a lot of care and love but feel free to reprimand or discipline them the way a parent would. They often use the formal "you" form (*usted* rather than *tu*) to address the younger children, thereby creating a greater distance in terms of status, authority, and respect.[6] The intense nature of these relationships at such an early age seems to generate exceptionally strong bonds among siblings.

Some children have greater responsibilities to their families, such as working outside the home to earn money to help support the family. Such work usually involves doing menial labor that only very poor people do, such as selling newspapers or gum on major boulevards in the middle of traffic. Not only does this type of work keep children from attending school on a regular basis, it also exposes them to high levels of engine exhaust fumes and places them in danger of getting hit by a car.

Children encounter other, more subtle risks on a daily basis. For example, an unhealthy activity popular among children is going to the store to buy candy and other forms of "junk" food such as soft drinks, chips, and white bread. In part, this may be their way of supplementing their meals, but unfortunately while these snacks curb their hunger, they offer little in the way of nutritional value. To make matters worse, the junk food tends to make children gain weight, thus creating the illusion that the children are healthy.[7] Another significant problem is the lack of potable water, considered the leading cause of gastroenteritis, especially among children, in Jocotán.[8] Other health risks include exposure to drugs, alcoholism, and gangs, which are exceptionally prevalent in Jocotán.

The risks children encounter in their daily lives underscore the indirect ways in which they experience the current social, economic, and political problems of domination. In more direct forms, children experience the dominant culture primarily through school, and to a lesser degree, through television and Catholic religious instruction. It is important to note that in a hegemonic system, the dominant culture uses state agencies and institutions, including the communications media, to inculcate values that serve its own political ends. Speaking of the Mexican educational system, however, Cockcroft notes both the rule and the exception:

> As agents of the state, the teachers are obligated to reproduce the dominant bourgeoisie ideology and to inculcate students with the virtues of *civismo* (good citizenship) and other values that will lead them to accept their given social position or chance. Yet historically teachers have earned their public "image" as defenders of social justice, and to the degree that they learn from students of poor people's complaints or improve the ability of young workers to analyze critically, they become important agents in the struggle to transform society. (1983, 215)

In theory, Jocoteños might hope to encounter a source of political and cultural support within the school system. But unfortunately, in practice, the elementary school in Jocotán exemplifies the corrupt and repressive aspect of the Mexican educational system.[9] Although state-funded education expanded significantly after the Mexican Revolution, scholars have shown that "education has not offered a significant exodus from poverty in the post-revolutionary period" because "the educational system most effectively serves the already privileged" (Vaughan 1982, 2). Emulating European and American models, post-revolutionary Mexican educators integrated the notion of European superiority into their own educational philosophy, blaming economic backwardness on the behavioral deficiencies of the Mexican. Hence, the educational system focused on removing such alleged deficiencies as "laziness, weakness, envy, alcoholism" from the Mexican character. As Vaughan notes, "Not surprisingly, this kind of racial categorization was often specifically directed toward the indigenous people and the working class" (Ibid., 172).

Even the textbooks reflect this preference of European over indigenous culture, as discussed in Chapter 3. History textbooks, at the height of the post-revolutionary nationalist wave, for example, portrayed the Spanish conquerors as "civilizers," thereby justifying the conquest of and subsequent violence against the native Mexicans (Vaughan 1982, 215–38).

Despite the nationalist, pro-indigenous, and egalitarian goals espoused by many Mexican revolutionaries, the texts reflected pre-revolutionary values and perspectives. They were in many ways racist, authoritarian, supportive of a clearly demarcated social hierarchy, and adulatory of imperialist powers (1982, 237). Fifty years later, Mexican textbooks show little improvement:

> When an Indian appears, he (she) is represented as an outsider, either as the former ruler of Mexico who practiced noble but strange customs, or as the poor humble Indian of the present who should be treated kindly by the Mestizo youngster and helped to assimilate. (Friedlander 1975, 147)

The view of Mexican history and nationalism promoted in the public schools is so critical to the state that it has been the subject of special conferences and debates.[10]

In addition to coping with textbooks that reinforce negative or romantic views of their indigenous heritage, the residents of Jocotán experience other problems with their local elementary school. This school lacks many necessary resources and facilities, such as sufficient and adequate desks, blackboards, drinking water, proper lighting, and janitorial service. However, parents express their greatest concern about the lack of the most fundamental educational resource, which is, of course, competent and dedicated teachers. The turnaround record for teachers in Jocotán is very high, which supports the claim by locals that most teachers accept a position in this community only until something better comes along. Several adult informants mentioned how they tried to get along with the local school teachers, in spite of conflicts, for fear that the teachers would get revenge on them by treating their children unfairly, even to the point of failing them. For example, two women told me that their nephew had been held back in the fourth grade for three years by the same teacher, *"porque le agarró mala idea"* ("because she took a dislike to him"). As the boy was actually quite bright, each year he became more bored, not to mention humiliated, and as a result, he became the class clown, thereby infuriating the teacher all the more. The situation became a vicious cycle and his family believed this was simply a strategy to force him out of school.[11] In such cases, unless the school principal happens to be extraordinarily sensitive to the community and takes the time to intervene in such matters, the parents and their children are virtually at the mercy of the overworked, poorly paid teachers.[12]

Yet, as mentioned in Chapter 4, most parents in Jocotán consider formal education an important part of childhood, and they encourage children to do well in school, as it offers one hope for achieving a better standard of living. Because of the many shortcomings of the local school, however, some parents opt to send their youngsters to schools in the surrounding *colonias*, or residential districts, of Guadalajara. Nevertheless, this alternative carries its own set of problems — not only do families have to spend more money on education and worry about getting their children to and from school each day,[13] they must also confront problems of social and class difference. Many parents have complained that their children experience negative peer pressure for being "*del pueblo*" or from the rural areas, a term which implies that they are country hicks. Jocoteño children are often labeled "*indios*" (Indians), or "*los pobres del pueblo*" (the poverty-stricken ones), while they respond to those remarks by calling city children "*los cremosos*" (roughly equivalent to the English phrase "cream of the crop"), a tongue-in-cheek reference to the latter's self-assigned superiority. The term *cremoso* neatly underscores the social distinctions based on race or color (white above brown). But even for children who attend school locally, the social differences between Jocoteños and city people are brought to their attention by the priest, the teachers, and other outsiders, who often look down upon the locals.

Like the school, the Catholic Church supports the dominant system, although one may find exceptions, particularly among those priests who advocate and practice the theology of liberation. But in Jocotán, as in many Mexican communities, the priests have tended to assume an authoritarian role.[14] The priest assigned to this community between 1980 and 1986 proved to be exceptionally rigid in terms of what he believed to be the correct and acceptable way of practicing Catholicism. The principal strategy for inculcating these values in the local community was to indoctrinate the children at a early age through catechism classes. To make this strategy more effective, the priest carefully chose and trained adults from within the community to teach catechism, according to his own specifications. In this way, the former priest created the impression that his views of Catholicism were (or should be) accepted by the community.

In addition to the Sunday masses and catechism classes, the priest also offered masses regularly at dawn and a rosary every afternoon. Interestingly, the priest presented the daily sunrise masses as special privileges that could be revoked if people did not comply with his demands. The fact that on Wednesdays, the sunrise mass was offered in a neighboring community, was not a valid excuse for absence. Instead, it only served to reinforce the priest's threat to offer his services elsewhere. Such despotic behavior induced children and other residents to constantly seek his approval or give up on him altogether. While the rosaries did not actually require the priest's presence, they nonetheless functioned to integrate children into sanctioned church activities, and therefore offered another way through which parishioners could demonstrate their obedience to the priest. As detailed in Chapter 7, those who did not succumb to his rule were ruthlessly banned from all church activities.

The current priest has developed a much stronger following than the previous priest because he has opted for gentle persuasion rather than rigid demands to influence the community, and because he is much more tolerant of local practices. Unlike his predecessor, this priest avoids extremist behavior in order to appeal to a broader spectrum of Catholics, that is, he allows for more personal expressions of religious faith, even if they depart somewhat from the official Catholic doctrine. For example, he tells parishioners that religious sentiments articulated in the Tastoanes festival are basically consistent with those prescribed by the church. However, he urges people to control their licentious behavior. Public drunkenness among festival participants, he argues, should not be tolerated, especially since minors make up a large percentage of those in attendance. By working to modify certain aspects of the festival, rather than to insist on abolishing the festival altogether, the current priest achieves a greater following. This compromise between the official and local ways better accommodates local religious beliefs and practices.

With respect to mass media, television is perhaps the most effective means for reaching children, since they spend little time reading books, newspapers, or magazines except for their school texts.[15] Through television, they get exposed to commercials and programs which promote the capitalist ideology of commodity consumption and "modernization."[16] One of the more subtle forms of influence, however, are the popular *telenovelas*, or soap operas, which often treat issues of ethnic and class differences in romantic and superficial ways. The impact of this genre in Mexico merits further consideration and has only recently attracted the attention of scholars (Straubhaar 1985, 115). But certain trends, such as the reification of light skin, do not escape the notice even of young children. Both on television and in their daily life, fair skin, and blue or green eyes are strongly associated with beauty. While children do not necessarily consider the combination of straight black hair, dark skin, and brown eyes as signs of ugliness, they often speak of these as features of Indianness, and are therefore less desired.

American films offer another source through which children get exposed to different ideologies. Since no movie theaters exist in Jocotán, children occasionally attend matinees in the city of Guadalajara. And, through advertisements on television and radio, kids are well informed about the latest commercial hits, or *lo que anda de moda*. Unfortunately, American motion pictures have predominantly presented very negative stereotypes of Mexicans, the most common of which are the violent bandit, the lazy peon, and, more recently, the gang member.[17] Reflecting on this very problem, a local teenager noted, *"siempre nos ponen de lo peor"* ("They always portray us as the worst").

While this particular teenager expressed resentment over what she considered to be unfair representations, less critical views are also common. Among teenagers, the United States is generally compared quite favorably to Mexico, especially with respect to clothing (fashion), music (modern rock), and technology. That such impressions are at least partially informed by American movies was made apparent in the children's conversations with me. After seeing *Karate Kid*, for example, the children informally discussed the movie with me, noting the excellent quality of the homes and the high standard of living presented in the film. Such observations underscore that American films undoubtedly make a strong impression on the children above and beyond the plot line and the intended message of the film.

In sum, the church, the school, and the media systematically devalue local practices and indio identity. In the best of situations, the church assumes a paternalistic attitude towards its parishioners who, with patience and persuasion, can be taught the right way to worship. The school offers few, if any, real opportunities for locals to acquire sufficient and necessary skills to improve their standard of living or to assume positions of community leadership. At the same time, the schools work to socialize children into the mainstream national culture by teaching them to identify with the nation-state rather than with their indigenous roots. Finally, the media naturalizes, if not glamorizes, mainstream transnational consumer tendencies, in which acquiring material goods becomes the hallmark of progress and modernity. Together, these forces of the dominant culture insure that "indio" culture remains a sign of backwardness, embarrassment, comedy, or the exotic past, but not a viable or desirable identity in the present.

Against this broadly defined Mexican cultural/political framework, Jocoteño children experience their local culture through their families and through established local traditions and practices developed within and maintained by the Jocoteño community such as fiestas, danzas, beliefs, local history, arrangement and use of space, etc. Most social activities are family oriented, and it is important to consider that children rarely leave Jocotán without supervision from a trusted adult. Even adolescents and young adults spend most of their leisure time in Jocotán. It is in this way that the significance of local expressive practices such as fiestas and danzas emerges. Such practices become the focal point of social interaction in Jocotán.

Children participate in La Fiesta de Los Tastoanes in various ways. Parents play a vital role in involving the very young children in the festival, for it is the parents who make a manda on behalf of their children. As early as age 1 or 2, parents dress their little boys as either Santiago or a Tastoan during the festival in fulfillment of the manda. By dressing in costume, children learn at an early stage in life to incorporate the identity represented by the costume into their own being. At this age, the children do not actually dance in the festival; rather, they attend mass, follow the procession, or simply observe the activities from the sidelines. As they get a little older, the children who must fulfill a manda are allowed to dance in the festival under the guidance of an older brother, uncle, or father. By age 12 or so, young boys may participate in the festival of their own free will. Rarely, however, do they dance throughout the entire event. Instead, three or more boys will take turns sharing the mask and costume, dancing for about one-hour periods.

Just as in the actual festival, it is primarily the boys who engage in Tastoanes games both during the festival and during the regular year. Boys will make milk-carton masks and use sticks or branches to play Tastoanes. The games can be as informal as a simple encounter with an imaginary opponent, or they can involve a large group of boys giving chase to Santiago on his bicycle. The variations are as endless as the children's imagination. One mother, showing me a mask made by her 6-year-old son, recalled:

> *Se agrarran jugando con palos y se sube mi hijo a la bicicleta y los demás bailandole alrededor. Según él, es el Santiago, juegan muy bonito estos chiquillos. A él le gusta mucho, dice que él va ser el Santiago cuando sea grande. Dice, "Yo voy a ser Santiago para pelearme con mi papa. Si me tumba, le doy un garrafón de vino." Es lo que dan, pero no sé, tiene mucha imaginación este niño. Le sale cada cosa!*

(They start fighting with sticks and he gets on his bicycle with the rest dancing around him. According to him, he's Santiago, they play beautifully. He likes it a lot and says that he's going to be Santiago when he grows up. He says "I am going to be Santiago to fight with my father. If he knocks me down, I'll give him a jug of liquor." That's what they give, but I don't know, he has a lot of [vivid] imagination. The things he thinks of!)[18]

It bears mentioning that children desire both the Santiago role and the Tastoanes roles because they each represent a source of power. Santiago represents power in terms of his ability to heal and help people, as well as in terms of the respect and honor he commands. On the other hand, the Tastoanes demonstrate their own power in terms of the freedom to break rules, to establish their own rules, and ultimately to define the game.

Kids also introduce novel ideas into the actual festival. For example, one year, tying a bandanna around the head in "cholo" fashion became a popular style introduced by the young teenagers as an identifying mark of their participation. Eventually, however, this fad was transformed by tying the bandanna around the nose of the mask, thereby incorporating it into the festival repertoire in a less challenging manner.

Masks also feature identifying trademarks from the youth, such as the names of current European and American rock bands, graffiti, or other trends that can't be easily disguised or incorporated by the adults. This example illustrates the constant tension and interplay between the dominant and local culture as children draw on various sources (national and transnational "youth" culture) to challenge their parents, even as they become incorporated into local culture.

As spectators, boys and girls participate in more equal numbers. Children observe virtually every single event. To get a better view, kids will climb trees, rooftops, walls, church towers, and other high places that have the additional advantage of providing protection from the crowds and the rowdy Tastoanes. Even though the younger children are often afraid of the Tastoanes, they refuse to stay home and miss the excitement.[19] Instead, they ask their parents or their older siblings to accompany them to the festival.

La Fiesta de los Tastoanes clearly constitutes one of the most important activities of local culture, but it is not the only one. La danza de los sonajeros represents another indigenous activity performed by Jocoteños for special religious festivities, including La Fiesta de los Tastoanes. Originally performed as a fertility dance, this dance has become symbolic of indigenous culture, making its performance a marker of indigenous identity, or more precisely, an expression of the desire to emphasize the indigenous roots of mestizo culture in public presentations. Rehearsals of this danza are held every night for at least two months before the scheduled performance, attracting participants and spectators alike. Most of the participants are approximately 14 to 30 years old, and it is the young children who make up the largest group of spectators. The latter often dance on the sidelines, eventually working themselves into the actual group of performers. The critical point for our present discussion is that during such activities, the community is drawn together to engage in one another's company (either as spectators or participants). In this way, local culture provides an alternative to participation in those domains controlled by the dominant culture.

Another aspect of local culture not controlled by the dominant culture is play time. Through play, children can experience the arbitrary nature of the rules under which they must live and, more importantly, enjoy the opportunity to explore and create other, alternative forms of existence. Particularly in the schools, where children encounter the dominant culture most directly, children are taught to not question authority, to not raise different points of view, and they learn very quickly that the teacher is the authority who has total control over their lives, at least within the school environment. On the other hand, play offers the children a creative outlet and develops concepts that are more akin to those promoted in La Fiesta de los Tastoanes. In their daily play activities, children are not bound to a set of explicit and rigid rules, other than those they create. Consequently, children always have the option of exercising their right not to play if they don't like the dynamics of a given game. Similarly, bossy kids could end up with no playmates if they push their weight around too much. This flexibility in defining the terms of their play activities encourages more negotiation among children.

In Chapter 1, I explained that as ritual clowns, the Tastoanes take the liberty of playing with social categories and cultural order during festival. By taking forms and elements of the familiar and rearranging them in novel combinations, they create a world of "make-believe." Such activities may encourage and therefore sharpen the participants' ability to think critically, to question, and simply to reflect upon those values, moral beliefs, and practices which are imposed upon them.

In this respect, playtime is like festival. Indeed, according to Huizinga (1955), play may be defined as occasions of questioning, speculation, and self-commentary. The key point is that playtime, like festival, encourages multiple dialogues and the development of alternative worlds — skills, concepts, and states of being not encouraged by the dominant culture. Scholars such as Turner, Wallace, and Babcock have noted that "the factors of one's culture are learned by experiencing them confused, inverted, rearranged. But more than simply reinforcing traditional relations and structures, such displacements and contradictions prompt speculation about, reflection on, and reconsideration of the order of things" (Babcock 1988, 122).

I have used the terms dominant and local culture as if they were two entirely distinct entities, but this is not so. Certainly, the rock band names and graffiti that teenager's paint on their Tastoanes mask, or the banda music performed for the mañanitas to Santiago and at the closing dance, provide clear examples of the interface between dominant and local culture. As Williams reminds us, and as the above discussion clearly demonstrates, the dominant culture tries to represent itself as *the* culture and contain all others within its range. Consequently, local forms of culture become subject to manipulation and appropriation. However, domination is never total or complete. Therefore, residual and emergent forms of culture, such as La Fiesta de los Tastoanes in Jocotán, exist in a constant tension as alternatives to the dominant culture. Oftentimes, conflict results from these competing enculturating processes, especially in light of the fact that parents place considerable weight on formal education. Youth gangs, who rebel against all social norms imposed upon them, can perhaps be best understood as a response to the confusion caused by such conflicts. While such contradictions are inherent in a hegemonic struggle, they further underscore the significance of active participation by children in local traditions.

How do we assess the significance and long-term implications of children's involvement in festival? To my knowledge, there are virtually no published studies on children in festival. However, general studies of children's folklore provide possible directions for the analysis of children's involvement in La Fiesta de los Tastoanes. In a recent survey of children's folklore, McDowell notes that much of children's folklore "constitutes a major enculturative forum paralleling the institutional educational process," although "school operates in quite a different manner, imposing a discipline and orientation extrinsic to the world of childhood" (1983, 321). In another study, however, Mechling warns against assuming that children are merely "unsocialized adults whose main goal is to acquire the adult world view" (1986, 93). Mechling's point is an important one: we must not limit our perception of children's folklore to its socializing potential. But taken at a more fundamental level, Mechling's warning also alerts us to the fact that the issue of socialization must not be taken for granted. Recalling Williams, within a hegemonic structure, socialization is a particularly complex process with important political implications.

McDowell's observation that children's folklore is an enculturating process holds some validity in Jocotán, except that he seems to equate the adult world and the dominant culture. As we have seen, in Jocotán, the two are not synonymous because school, an institution controlled by the dominant culture, imposes a social and cultural worldview that is in many instances extrinsic to the Jocoteño adult world as well. Thus, children's participation in folklore or "local culture" enculturates them into the Jocoteño adult world, whereas school enculturates children into the dominant culture.

From this perspective, children's participation in festival and their play based on the festival is doubly important. From the description of both the daily lives of the children and their involvement in the festival, it is clear that many of the patterns observed in children's behavior at the festival correspond to their everyday relationships and roles within the local Jocoteño culture. As such, the festival further reinforces those established patterns and paves the way for their future participation as adults. Furthermore, early participation in the festival provides an important avenue through which children may become part of the traditional community. Not only does early participation in the festival encourage the existing traditional community to accept the children into their circle, regardless of a child's parents' status, but it provides the children an opportunity to fully experience a sense of belonging to that community. Additionally, La Fiesta de los Tastoanes provides one means through which children can examine Jocoteño historical, religious, and cultural beliefs through concrete manifestations. In other words, abstract concepts, such as reciprocity or Santiago's healing power, are articulated in concrete form through festival, making use of all senses and thus engaging children to fully experience their local culture. In short, La Fiesta de los Tastoanes offers one important expressive means through which Jocoteño children learn about their world and, in turn, articulate their vision of the world. Thus, the festival appeals to children for several reasons: first, they find the festival period exciting and entertaining, since many outsiders visit the community; there is an abundance of food; certain restrictions are relaxed during this time (e.g., children may stay up later than usual); they often get new clothes, and even classes are disrupted on occasion. Moreover, the ties to a pre-Hispanic past are strengthened through festival performance, thereby adding a cosmological dimension to this period. But perhaps the two most attractive features of the festival are (1) the sense of challenging the "official" view on matters of history, religion, and politics, since the school, church, and mass media generally teach a different perspective than that expressed in the festival, and (2) the immediacy and direct relevance that dramatic enactment holds for the Jocoteños. While children are exposed to various enculturating processes and forms, festival is one of the only forms which demands total absorption (mind, body, spirit) and which exploits all the senses. The excitement and immediacy of festival participation is difficult to surpass.

Conclusion

Through festival, as well as through some of their play activities, Jocoteños articulate a worldview that counters that imposed upon them by the dominant culture. For many adult participants, one of the main reasons stated for actively participating in the festival is to honor their ancestors as an act of respect for those traditions that are constantly threatened by the hegemonic forces. Maintaining this tradition, in spite of opposition from the church and other officials, is a value that has been instilled in the children, as their involvement clearly demonstrates. Because the forces of socialization are multiple and often contradictory, it is difficult to determine what the future holds for these children and the festival. Nonetheless, their involvement in festival at this early age surely keeps alive their potential to see beyond the boundaries imposed by the dominant culture.

NINE

Summary and Conclusion

✦

In this final chapter, I summarize the central issues expressed in La Fiesta de los Tastoanes. First is the issue of identity: I have argued that the issue of identity figures centrally in La Fiesta de los Tastoanes of Jocotán, and that we must understand identity as a process subject to manipulation rather than as a static bounded category.

Clearly, the Jocoteño identity involves at least the symbolic recognition of an indigenous heritage. Participation in the Tastoanes festival — an expressive form that has been passed down through the generations — provides a way of symbolically affirming a link with the indigenous inhabitants of preconquest Jocotán. In fact, most families who have long histories in the community consider the Tastoanes festival a sacred tradition that must be maintained, in part as a form of respect and honor to their ancestors. For these reasons, the "most Jocoteño" members of the Jocotán community are the Tastoanes mayores because of their commitment to preserve La Fiesta de los Tastoanes in Jocotán.

For newcomers, participation in the festival provides a means through which they may demonstrate their interest in and respect for the established norms and values of Jocotán and ultimately become incorporated into the community. Novices initially learn through observation and participation in lesser roles, thereby demonstrating their commitment to and understanding of the festival. Consequently, as discussed in Chapter 8, children raised in Jocotán have the best possibility for establishing themselves as Jocoteños, regardless of their parents' status.

Yet outsiders obliterate local distinctions of identity by assigning the label of *indio*, intended usually in the most negative sense, to all residents of

Jocotán. In contemporary Mexico, the term *indio* has become a loaded and complex concept and usually carries derogatory connotations.[1] By reducing the issue of indigenous identity to a condition determined by geography, the politics of identity become further obscured. However, Jocoteños provide an alternative and much richer articulation of what it means to be "indio" through the Tastoanes festival, emphasizing that the indio identity is intimately tied to issues of authority and struggles against domination.

The connection between residency and identity is specially significant as outsiders increasingly encroach on the borders, and indeed into the very heart of the community of Jocotán. These constant invasions threaten the community in various ways. The former priest is one outsider who showed little regard for the people of Jocotán and their traditional practices and sought to change the community. The local schoolteachers constitute another group of outsiders who generally express little interest in, or support for, local traditions, and who work to replace them with those sanctioned by government officials at the national level.

El Sapo and his family represent another strong force in Jocotán who work to undermine the sense of communal pride and unity and clearly demonstrate that not all threats to the community derive from outside forces. As alleged practitioners of black magic, Los Sapos exert pressure on local residents to get what they want. Their biggest demand, however, is quite complicated, as it involves the return of some lands which they claim were wrongly sold to other residents. Sorting out these claims promises to be a long and complicated process.

El Sapo is not the only Jocoteño caught up in land rights negotiations. On the contrary, the dispute over land rights affects many residents of Jocotán, who have inherited land from their ancestors, for they have no written documents to prove ownership. In this way, tracing their indigenous heritage may prove important as a means of keeping their land. The festival not only links them with an indigenous past, but also asserts that the indios represent the original and therefore rightful owners of the territory. On the whole, La Fiesta de los Tastoanes makes clear that the indio identity is inseparable from issues of territory and domination, issues that are virtually ignored in official discourse and issues of vital concern for many Jocoteños today. For the "others" continue to dominate them, ignore or dismiss their local customs (especially of land ownership and local forms of religious expression), and ultimately continue to invade their territory in the broadest terms. Complaining about the rapid increase of outsiders moving into Jocotán, one man told me: *"Vienen y quieren cambiar todo. Ya es más fácil que lo saquen a uno que uno a ellos."* ("They come and want to change everything. Now its easier for them to kick us [old-time residents] out than for us to keep them out.")

By now it should be clear that although the Tastoanes festival symbolically represents a central aspect of Jocoteño identity and ideology, Jocotán is not a homogeneous community, as evidenced by the local phrase, *"Somos cuatro y cada quien jala a su esquina"* ("We are four and each pulls to his own corner"). That is, while Jocoteños as a community may uphold certain values or ideals, they often disagree in terms of how to achieve them. The greatest cause of conflict, in my judgment, has to do with the future of Jocotán. On the one hand, the luxuries of modern technology available in the newly established colonias on the borders of Jocotán bring into sharper focus the impoverished living conditions of Jocotán. Yet, while some residents would like to bring such improvements as running water, telephone, and postal service into Jocotán, others are reluctant to cooperate towards such efforts for fear that the expenses incurred will be too high and also because it will make Jocotán even more attractive to outsiders. In addition, the bureaucratic red tape involved in making such technological changes is convoluted enough to discourage anyone from such a major undertaking. One strategy for improving Jocotán while maintaining its present character is to have the government recognize this community as a historical site for preservation. This strategy involves demonstrating that Jocotán is an ancient Indian community. Nonetheless, only a small minority (essentially the local DIF representatives) really supports this historical preservation effort and until a larger support base is established, nothing can really be done.

Since the Tastoanes festival attests to the indigenous roots of the town, it figures prominently in the debate concerning the future of Jocotán. In recent years, La Fiesta de los Tastoanes has attracted the attention of news reporters, state agency officials, and a few researchers affiliated with universities and other research institutions. The response to this attention has been as mixed as the reasons for researching the festival. Two newspaper reports exemplify the broad range of reports on the festival. In one, a brief description of the 1985 festival was published by a local folklorist in a major city newspaper, highlighting activities for each day of the festival.[2] Because this report appeared in the cultural section of the newspaper the day before the festival began (September 7), with instructions on how to find Jocotán, the objective seemed to be to attract residents of Guadalajara to witness the festival. In another report, a somewhat leftist newspaper from the Universidad Autónoma de Guadalajara, devoted an entire page, featuring five color photographs, to the Tastoanes festival of Jocotán.[3] Approximately one-half of the text was devoted to giving background and description of the festival, while the other half dealt with the numerous problems affecting Jocoteños. Regarding the first half, the newspaper reported that Jocotán is "an indigenous community which has been absorbed by the city of Guadalajara and is presently considered a colonia of the Zapopan." One of the main organizers of the festival is also quoted, stating that in the old days larger numbers of people participated actively in the festival but today a smaller number is involved because many people are no longer given permission to miss work for this festival. This information sets the tone for the second part of the report, in which various problems (insufficient water, lack of a drainage system, etc.) are discussed by local residents. The intention here was to promote public sympathy by showcasing this traditional town as a victim of modernity. Despite obvious good intentions, Jocoteños were upset by the report because one of the local residents took advantage of the attention to take personal credit for some of the improvements accomplished through community efforts. Furthermore, in both reports, Jocoteños were unhappy to find details that were not quite accurate.

Typically, Jocoteños do not read the daily newspapers, but on the days in which the Tastoanes festival was featured, newspaper vendors from Guadalajara appeared in Jocotán waving the reports. These newspaper reports highlight two things: (1) that the festival is the one thing that can draw public attention to Jocotán, and (2) that this attention can be manipulated toward various ends. But, above all, the reports underscore the lack of real communication between Jocoteños and outsiders. Many of the errors and distortions are caused by doing superficial, impressionistic reporting, which indicates a lack of commitment from reporters who do not take the time to really know the community and assess the problems thoroughly. Since I walked around with a camera frequently, a few people, suspecting I was a newspaper reporter, complained to me about the newspaper write-ups.

Despite the discrepancies and shortcomings, many Jocoteños enjoy the media attention. The recent documentation of the 1987 Tastoanes festival by a local television station posed a serious question: was this an initial effort by the dominant culture to commodify the festival for tourist consumption and thereby minimize its contestative potential? Jocotan's proximity to Guadalajara (a major tourist destination) and Mexico's history of commercializing its folk and popular traditions would certainly support this possibility.[4] Certainly, my most recent visit in 1991 attests to the fact that an increasing number of "outsiders," i.e., scholars and tourists, are coming to the festival. I have already noted how the church, school, and other agents of the state operate to control the people of Jocotán. From this perspective, at least some of the recent media attention can be interpreted as yet another form of encroachment by the dominant culture.

Conclusion

Previous studies of Mexican festival have focused too narrowly on one aspect or another, resulting in a limited understanding of this complex phenomenon. Severely lacking is a detailed account of what the festival is about, and why and how people participate in the festival. Throughout this study, I have argued that festival has to be understood as a complex, multidimensional social process. After describing the festival, I sought to provide a more holistic understanding of festival by examining La Fiesta de los Tastoanes as a local way of constituting and re-enacting the past. I showed how the festival generates multiple interpretations that relate to the social and political history of Jocotán. Through both oral accounts and the enactment of the Tastoanes festival, Jocoteños draw on the past as a metaphor to articulate the sense of invasion and domination that constitutes their daily reality. In sum, the history and analysis of La Fiesta de los Tastoanes provided in this study demonstrates that this festival is both an event that is intricately linked to the lives of the Jocoteños, as well as a dynamic process through which their lives are linked to one another. Hence, the festival has been and continues to be the focal point of Jocoteño life, bringing together the multiple facets and dimensions of social life in this community.

Based on the analysis presented in this study, one conclusion is evident: in Jocotán, La Fiesta de los Tastoanes has consistently played a role in the struggle for hegemony. During the colonial period, in order to achieve their goal of conversion and domination, the Spanish missionaries infused indigenous ritual celebrations with Spanish Christian religious elements that were heavily laden with Spanish cultural and political ideals. However, it was precisely the indigenous base of these syncretic religious practices that allowed the native Mexicans the means through which they could perpetuate their own residual beliefs and practices and thereby resist the conquerors' subjugating practices. This process of hybridization, which produced La Fiesta de los Tastoanes, made the festival a critical site of hegemonic struggle. But hybridization also enabled Jocoteños to make use of all resources available, including those imposed or otherwise introduced by outsiders, in order to adapt to the changing circumstances over the years while simultaneously striving to maintain their indigenous identity. Hence, La Fiesta de los Tastoanes constitutes a major site for the articulation of indigenous perspectives concerning ideology and identity. So it is that from its formative years to the present, the Tastoanes festival has been an important arena in which political, religious, economic, and cultural aspects of domination have been articulated, negotiated, and challenged.

Notes

1. Officially, the patron saint of Jocotán is Ascensión, but residents do not honor him with a special celebration on his saint's day, which falls on August 15.

2. Important contributors to these concepts include Abrahams (1977, 1981); Geertz (1973); and Bauman (1986).

3. The term *residual*, as employed by Williams, must not be confused with the term *survival*, though both evoke the notion of "stagnant residue." To avoid confusion, I prefer to use the term *indigenous culture*, especially in colonial situations in which new cultures are literally imposed upon the local indigenous population.

4. Numerous scholars have examined and theorized the concept of hybridization. For further discussion, see Garcia-Canclini (1987), Anzaldua (1987), and Rosaldo (1990).

5. Today, variations of this dance–drama may be found throughout Spain and its former colonies around the world. See, for example, Kurath (1949b) and Warman (1972).

6. Jocoteños, like all Mexicans, are mestizos because they are people of mixed Spanish and indigenous ancestry. Their social identity, however, is a more complex matter which will be taken up in later chapters.

7. Classic studies include Blaffer (1972), Bricker (1973, 1981), Brandes (1990), Cancian (1965), Ingham (1986), Gossen (1974), Warren (1978), Vogt (1969), Erasmus (1961), de la Peña (1981), and Watanabe (1992).

8. See, for example, Blaffer (1972), Buchler (1967), Cancian (1965, 1967), Carrasco (1961), Crumrine, L. (1969), Crumrine, N. (1970), Crumrine, L. and Crumrine, N. (1977), DeWalt (1975), Erasmus (1961), Friedlander (1981), Nash (1968), Smith (1977), Tax (1953), Vogt (1965), and Wolf (1957).

9. Watanabe (1992) offers an excellent overview of the Mesoamerican literature on Maya identity.

10. Also referred to as the fiesta system. For detailed reviews, see Greenberg (1981) and Smith (1977).

11. Marianne Mesnil has noted that traditional festivals are produced by and for community members, while in modern societies festivals are produced by some for the consumption of others (Mesnil 1987).

12. For detailed reviews of these debates, see Watanabe (1992), Greenberg (1981), and Walderman Smith (1977).

13. Here, I am referring only to the literature on cargo systems.

14. See, for example, Bricker (1973), Blaffer (1977), Crumrine, L. (1969), and Nash (1968).

CHAPTER ONE

1. Visual documentation of the festival by means of photography and video cameras has become increasingly common as the festival attracts more scholars and reporters. But locals, too, have turned to mechanical means of reproducing the festival as a way to share the festival with their extended families and friends residing in the United States.

2. The literature on this topic is abundant. For example, see Clifford and Marcus (1986).

3. See Bauman (1986) for a discussion of Burke's contribution to cultural performance theory.

4. See Ong (1982, 1–9).

5. See also Hill (1988) and Wolf (1982).

6. Standard views on the Spanish–indigenous encounter tend to emphasize the "civilizing, Christianizing" goals, while minimizing, or at least justifying, the land grabbing, enslaving aspects of the conquest. For details, see Chapters 3 and 8.

7. I believe that the reyes' role, which alludes to femininity, combined with the passive or non-violent approach to conflict, is meant to historically represent the Queen of Tonalá, who, recognizing her people could not defeat the Spanish invaders, opted to receive the Spaniards in peace. However, the androgynous character of the reyes may stem from the pre-Hispanic religious tradition which includes male, female, and androgynous symbols.

8. On the first day of the festival the Tastoanes succeed in killing Santiago. Resurrected by God, however, Santiago becomes invincible and untouchable thereafter.

9. The prevalence of brass bands throughout Latin America has undoubtedly contributed to the widespread popularity of the current "banda craze" among Latinos in the United States and Mexico. However, the newer bandas have developed distinctive trends in terms of costuming, style of playing, and dancing.

10. Las Mañanitas is a traditional Mexican song played for individuals celebrating their birthday or saint's day.

11. According to my informants, at one time a written text was available, but it has been lost for well over twenty years.

12. According to Mexican tradition, waving a branch or a bunch of weeds over a body is popularly believed to restore a lost or dying soul.

CHAPTER TWO

1. See, for example, Paredes (1977), Said (1978), and Clifford and Marcus (1986).

2. But see Aguilar (1981), Fahim (1982), Jones (1970), Ohnuki-Tierney (1984), Vigil (1990), and Zavella (1987).

3. For recent work in this area, see Kondo (1986), Limón (1990), and Nayaran (1993).

4. Ohnuki-Tierney (1984) notes that the "temporary" nature of an ethnographer's fieldwork in a given community contributes to his/her "outsider" status.

5. The names of my informants have been changed to protect their identities.

6. Negotiating prices, especially within the family domain, is considered a very delicate and private matter. My hostess basically told me that I did not have to pay her anything, which put me in an awkward situation because I did not want to insult her generosity but neither did I want to take advantage of her. I resolved this issue by telling her that my research grant included a stipend to cover my living expenses and paid her based on the going rate in the city for renting a room, which she found acceptable.

7. Since money matters are considered very private, I could not pursue this line of inquiry with regard to personal business transactions or festival sponsorship.

8. See Chapter 9 for more details regarding newspaper reports.

9. Jocotán has a long-standing reputation of being a rowdy community prone to violence, especially against outsiders (Colección de Acuerdos 1868, Tomo III: 184).

10. The appropriate title for a married woman is señora. To call a single woman "señora" is to imply that she is sexually active (i.e., not a virgin) and, thus, immoral. The term *seño*, roughly equivalent to the term *Ms.*, is often used to avoid a *faux pas*.

11. When I returned to Jocotán in September of 1991, most people expressed great pleasure (and relief) that I brought along my husband and baby daughter. Their presence helped affirm the claims I had made about my personal life, especially since my daughter spoke only Spanish and my husband helped me take care of the baby and conduct fieldwork. The fact that both my daughter and husband enjoyed the experience became readily apparent, and as a result, they were quickly welcomed in the community.

12. The problem of how to best do ethnographic writing has been a subject of great debate in anthropology. For a recent review of the subject, see James Clifford (1988), especially Chapter 1.

CHAPTER THREE

1. Gerhard also refers to Jocotán by the names San Gaspar, Xoxocotlán, and Jocotán de los Cedazos (1982, 133).

2. Lopez Portillo y Weber (1935, 38) claims that the term *Chimalhuacán* was never in fact really used by anyone, though it remains useful among scholars.

3. This word becomes important as the antecedent of the word *Tastoanes*. It bears emphasizing that gender was not inscribed in the term *tlatoani*.

4. All translations of Spanish texts are my own unless otherwise noted.

5. The existence of female, male, and androgynous symbols in pre-Hispanic religion lends support to my idea that indigenous cultures tended to accept and encompass difference. The androgynous reyes in the Tastoanes festival may be rooted in this pre-Hispanic notion.

6. Hunt (1977, 55) suggests that many pre-Hispanic religions were truly pantheistic in which God was both the one and the many, a theory which would account for the great number of deities as well as for the integration of Christian saints into indigenous religious practices.

7. Some writers refer to her as the *casica*, *señora*, or *tlatoani* (Lopez Portillo y Weber 1935).

8. For a discussion concerning the issue of polygamy with regards to Christianity, see Ricard (1966, 110–11). See also Trexler (1982, 119).

9. For a good discussion on this topic, see León-Portillo (1975), especially Chapter 5.

10. Boletín de la Junta Auxiliar Jalisciense (1941–2, 139)

11. According to Gerhard (1982, 132), within Tala the political units at contact were Tlallán, Ocotlán, Cuyupuztlán, and Ixtlán.

12. This community was founded by Viceroy de Mendoza.

13. Analco was founded by the Franciscans, who owned a convent in the indigenous town of Tetlán, which they relocated west of San Juan de Dios River along with it indigenous inhabitants.

14. According to Richard Harris and David Barkin (1982), as a result of the increasing commercialization of agriculture, the production of cash crops for export and industrial use has expanded at the expense of the production of basic food crops needed by the population. Insufficient land and capital have forced many peasants to seek wage employment. As a result of new policies, even ejido and communal lands can now be "associated with the land owned by individuals and/or agribusiness in order to permit the introduction of large amounts of capital and modern technology to increase productivity." Yet, in the process, the peasants will become little more than a cheap labor force working their own lands.

15. For a concise overview on Mexican immigration, see Adler Helman (1983, 108–12).

16. Wolf explains that wealthy mestizos could actually obtain legal documents identifying them as "white" (1964, 236).

17. I am borrowing Peacock's terminology here (for an elaboration on this concept, see Chapter 4). Scott's concept of moral economy is also relevant (1976).

CHAPTER FOUR

1. Indeed, Cockcroft (1983, 3) notes that approximately half of the Mexican population lacks essential services such as potable drinking water, sewage services, and toilets.

2. Indice Alfabético de los Lugares Habitados del Estado de Jalisco, 1910.

3. Sexto Censo de Población (1943, 246); Séptimo Censo de Población (1952, 328); Octavo Censo de Población (1963, 151).

4. Noveno Censo General Población (1973, 290).

5. Estudio de Participación (1986).

6. In Mexico the state is divided into municipalities consisting of several townsites and ranchos and headed by a *presidente municipal*. The presidente municipal appoints a delegado municipal from within each town to represent his respective community for a three-year term.

7. Estudio de Participación Ciudadano (1986).

8. Ibid.

9. Toads are commonly associated with black magical practices in folklore.

10. Cholo refers to a subcultural style of dress and behavior associated with barrio gangs, as well as to individuals who assume that style, whether or not they belong to a gang. This term may have gained popularity as a result of heightened interaction with and exposure to Chicano youths due to increased immigration to the United States.

11. A few elder women have been very active in promoting and participating in the local customs, especially La Fiesta de los Tastoanes, but, despite their knowledge, age, and involvement, women are not generally included under the term Tastoanes mayores.

CHAPTER FIVE

1. Ascensión Gomez (1982).

2. For more information concerning Catholic religious practices in Spain at the time of the conquest, see Marzal (1993).

3. While Jocotán is not a peasant group, the basic concept advanced by Scott is nonetheless applicable to this society.

4. Ortner defines summarizing key symbols as "those symbols which are seen as summing up, expressing, representing for the participants in an emotionally powerful and relatively undifferentiated way, what the system means to them. . . . It does not encourage reflection on the logical relations among these ideas, nor on theological consequences of them as they are played out over time and history. . . . They operate to compound and synthesize a complex system of ideas." (1973, 1338)

5. For specific references, see Fletcher (1984, 53–77).

6. For general works on Santiago in Spain, see Kendrick (1960), Starkie (1965),

and Stone (1927). For references concerning Santiago in Mexico, see Warman (1977), Valle (1949), and Canto-Lugo (1991).

7. For an extensive bibliography on the moros y cristianos, consult Canto Lugo (1991).

8. A crusade is a military expedition undertaken by the Christian powers in the eleventh, twelfth, and thirteenth centuries to win the Holy Land from the Muslims.

9. Silverblatt (1988) has also discovered indigenous appropriations of Santiago among the Andean peoples of Peru.

10. Comaroff and Comaroff (1991) and Ranger (1975) note the manipulation of symbols as a central feature of colonial relationships.

11. A great deal of work by symbolic anthropologists and performance-oriented folkloristics has centered around this point. For good reviews on this subject, see Schneider (1977), Bauman (1977, 1983), and Bauman and Abrahams (1981).

CHAPTER SIX

1. Klor de Alva claims that reciprocal exchange systems between deities and humans constitute a core aspect of indigenous religious beliefs and practices (1980, 80).

2. Appropriately, Bourdieu terms such gains "symbolic profit" and considers them as a form of credit (1990, 120). In the broadest sense, symbolic profit contributes to one's "credibility."

3. The weaving together of moral, economic, social, and religious sanctions is common among peasants living by the subsistence ethic or moral economy (Scott 1976, 6).

4. On this point, see Cook (1973), Appadurai (1988), and Bourdieu (1990).

5. Whether or not ritual gifting, especially the prenda exchange system, figured prominently in pre-Hispanic cultures is insignificant. In Williams's terms, ritual gifting could be an emergent, or "invented," tradition and still retain its ideological significance.

CHAPTER SEVEN

1. Chapters 3 and 8 are particularly relevant in this regard.

2. Although the theme of hybridization has been addressed from a variety of perspectives, my view is closest to that articulated by Anzaldua, who explains: "La mestiza constantly has to shift out of habitual formations; from convergent thinking, analytical reasoning that tends to use rationality to move toward a single goal (a Western mode), to divergent thinking, characterized by movement away from set patterns and goals and toward a more whole perspective, one that includes rather than excludes" (1987, 79).

3. Abrahams (1977, 1981) introduced the notion of cultural enactment to refer to any framed, symbolically rich cultural activity such as festival.

4. See Chapter 1 for a detailed description of the Spanish Christians and the Tastoanes.

5. My work contrasts sharply with Todorov (1984), both in terms of theoretical approaches and especially in our conclusions. For a good critique of Todorov's book, see Root (1988), who summarizes Todorov's argument as follows: "Todorov's understanding of the radical difference between 'Indian' and European culture rests on three interrelated notions he believes pre-Columbian native society exhibits: a concept of time which was almost completely past-oriented, a profound social conformity, and a cultural stasis which rendered change nearly impossible. These qualities, he asserts, ultimately 'explain' the Mexican defeat" (1988, 201).

6. Bauman (1987) illustrates how seventeenth century Quakers conceived of festival as synonymous with a lifestyle that contradicted their own.

7. See Allon White (1986, 1987) for detailed discussion on this point.

8. I am indebted to Beverly Stoeltje for calling this point to my attention.

9. Taped interview, August 1986.

10. By attacking these delivery trucks, which represent large corporations, the Tastoanes demonstrate that they can invert the power structure and take control — at least during festival. In this way, they symbolically draw attention to the boundaries that distinguish them from the dominant world.

11. See also Brandes (1988, 175–78) for additional information on ritual drinking.

CHAPTER EIGHT

1. See Trexler (1982) for a discussion of the important role young Indian boys played in evangelizing other Mexican natives.

2. Television soap operas were discussed more frequently among children than were cartoons. The early afternoons feature soap operas designed for young children, such as the popular *Carusel* (Carousal) or *Mundo de Juguetes* (World of Toys), whose protagonists are young children.

3. The number of students cited in the census refers only to children attending elementary school in Jocotán proper. It does not account for preschoolers or residents of Santa Maria de Jocotán.

4. Martin provides an excellent case study of "school failure" in Mexico (1994).

5. Martin has observed that self-regulating families (i.e., families living on hand-to-mouth existence) must depend on all members to contribute to the family's well-being (1994, 114).

6. Adults will often employ the *usted* form with very young children to teach them to respond using the *usted* form.

7. There is a tendency among Mexicans to assume that being "*gordito*," or chubby, is a sign of being well-fed and therefore healthy.

8. Estudio de Participación Ciudadano (1986).

9. For recent case studies concerning the quality of education in Jalisco, Mexico, see Martin (1994).

10. For an overview of nationalism and education in Mexico, see Josefina Vasquez de Knauth (1970).

11. Martin's study (1994) documents that the humiliation of a student is a common disciplinary mode employed by teachers in this municipio.

12. Martin succinctly explains the failure of schools in Mexico as follows: "To put it rather crudely, the parents, already hard-pressed by low and irregular incomes, which limit the attention available to the individual needs of the children's studies, find that the school, also constrained by limited resources and time, either neglects their children or off-load what appear to be disproportionate amounts of work and responsibility on to the parents. . . . The child is left suspended between the relations of mutual repulsion, and thus becomes a potential failure." (1994, 13)

13. Parents expressed great concern over the fact that the major boulevard that runs alongside Jocotán has no crosswalks, overpasses, or marked bus stops to ensure the safety of the children.

14. For other examples, see Ingham (1986, 47–54).

15. Cockcroft notes, "As only 2 percent of Mexico's population reads books, and lesser numbers consult the leftist press, the main media of communication have become television and, to a lesser degree, radio" (1983, 281).

16. See Mattelart (1985) and Corella (1985).

17. For historical summaries regarding the portrayal of Mexicans, see Woll (1980), Hadley-Garcia (1990), and Pettit (1980).

18. Taped interview, August 1986.

19. During the year, parents will often use the Tastoanes as bogeyman to help discipline their children. Bauman (1972) notes that belsnickles are used in a similar fashion in Nova Scotia.

CHAPTER NINE

1. For a detailed discussion on this subject, see Friedlander (1985).

2. "La Fiesta de Tastuanes en Jocotán," *El Informador* (Guadalajara), 7 September 1986, Suplemento Cultural, p. 16.

3. "Los Tastoanes, una Viva Tradición en Jocotán," *Metrópoli Ocho Columnas* (Guadalajara), 10 September 1986, p. 8B.

4. Brandes (1988, Chapter 5) provides an example in which the Mexican government has commercialized a traditional fiesta for its own financial and political gain.

Selected Bibliography

Abrahams, Roger D.
1981   Shouting Match at the Border: The Folklore of Display Events. In *"And Other Neighborly Names": Social Process and Cultural Image in Texas Folklore.* Richard Bauman and Roger D. Abrahams, eds. Pp. 303–321. Austin: University of Texas Press.

1977   Toward an Enactment-Centered Theory of Folklore. In *Frontiers of Folklore.* William Bascom, ed. Pp. 79–120. Boulder: Westview Press for the AAAS.

Aguilar, John L.
1981   Insider Research: An Ethnography of a Debate. In *Anthropologists at Home in North America: Methods and Issues in the Study of One's Own Society.* D. A. Messerschmidt, ed. Pp. 15–26. Cambridge: Cambridge University Press.

Aguirre Beltrán, Gonzalo
1946   *La Población Negra de Mexico, 1519–1810.* Mexico: Ediciones Fuentes Cultura.

Anzaldua, Gloria
1987   *Borderlands: The New Mestiza.* San Francisco, CA: Spinsters/Aunt Lute.

Arregui, Domingo Lázaro de
1980   *Descripción de la Nueva Galicia.* Guadalajara, Jalisco, Mexico: Gobierno de Jalisco, Secretaría General, Unidad Editorial.

Babcock, Barbara
1984   Arrange Me into Disorder: Fragments and Reflection on Ritual Clowning. In *Rites, Drama, Festival, Spectacle: Rehearsals Toward a Theory of Cultural Performance.* John J. MacAloon, ed. Pp. 102–128. Philadelphia: Institute for the Study of Human Issues.

1978   Introduction. In *The Reversible World.* Barbara Babcock, ed. Pp. 13–36. Ithaca: Cornell University Press.

Bakhtin, Mikhail M.
1981   Forms of Time and the Chronotype in the Novel. In *The Dialogic Imagination.* Michael Holquist, ed. Pp. 84–258. Austin: University of Texas Press.

1965   *Rabelais and His World.* Cambridge: MIT Press.

Baring-Gould, The Reverend S.
1914   *Lives of the Saints.* Vol. 8, Part 2. Edinburg: Ballantyne Press.

Bauman, Richard
1987   The Place of Festival in the Worldview of the Seventeenth Century Quakers. In *Time Out of Time.* Alessandro Falassi, ed. Pp. 93–98. Albuquerque: University of New Mexico Press.

1986   Performance and Honor in 13th Century Iceland. *Journal of American Folklore* 99:131–150.

1983   The Field Study of Folklore in Context. In *Handbook of American Folklore.* Richard Dorson, ed. Pp. 362–368. Bloomington: Indiana University Press.

1972   Belsnickling in a Nova Scotia Island Community. *Western Folklore* 31:229–243.

Bauman, Richard, and Roger D. Abrahams
1978   Ranges of Festival Behavior. In *The Reversible World.* Barbara Babcock, ed. Pp. 193–208. Ithaca: Cornell University Press.

Befu, Harumi
1977   Social Exchange. In *Annual Review of Anthropology* 6:255–282.

Bell, Betty
1974   *The Archeology of West Mexico.* Ajijic, Jalisco: Sociedad de Estudios Avanzados del Occidente de Mexico, A.C.

1971   Archeology of Nayarit, Jalisco and Colima. In *The Handbook of Middle American Indians* 11:694–753. Austin: University of Texas Press.

Blaffer, Sarah C.
1972   *The Black-man of Zinacantan.* Austin: University of Texas Press.

Bourdieu, Pierre
1990   *The Logic of Practice.* Stanford: Stanford University Press.

Brand, Donald
1971   Ethnohistoric Synthesis of Western Mexico. In *Handbook of Middle American Indians* 11:632–655. Austin: University of Texas Press.

Brandes, Stanley
1988   *Power and Persuasion: Fiestas and Social Control in Rural Mexico.* Philadelphia: University of Pennsylvania Press.

1983   The Posadas in Tzintzuntzan: Structure and Sentiment in a Mexican Christmas Festival. *Journal of American Folklore* 96:259–280.

1981   Cargos versus Cost Sharing in Mesoamerican Fiestas with Special Reference to Tzintzuntzan. *Journal of Anthropological Research* 37:209–225.

1981   Fireworks and Fiestas: The Case from Tzintzuntzan. *Journal of Latin American Lore* 7(2):171–190.

Brenner, Anita
1929   *Idols Behind Altars.* New York: Payson and Clarke, Ltd.

Bricker, Victoria Reifler
1981   *The Indian Christ, the Indian King.* Austin: University of Texas Press.

1973   *Ritual Humor in Highland Chiapas.* Austin: University of Texas Press.

Broderick, Robert C.
1976   *The Catholic Encyclopedia.* Nashville: Thomas Nelson, Inc.

Buchler, Ira
1967   La organización ceremonial de una aldea mexicana. *América Indígena* 27(2):237–263.

Burke, Kenneth
1957   *The Philosophy of Literary Form.* Vintage Books: Knopf and Random House.

Burke, Peter
1978 *Popular Culture in Early Modern Europe*. London: P. Smith.

Butler, Alban
1956 *Lives of the Saints*. Edited, revised and supplemented by Herbert Thuston, S.J., P. J. Kennedy, and Donald Attwater. Vol. 3. July, August and September. London: Burnes and Oates.

Campa, Arthur L.
1967 El Origen y la Naturaleza del Drama Folklorico. *Folklore Américas* 20(2):13–48.

Cancian, Frank
1967 Political and Religious Organizations. In *Handbook of Middle American Indians*. Robert Wachope and Manning Nash, ed. 6:238–298. Austin: University of Texas Press.

1965 *Economics and Prestige in a Maya Community*. Stanford: Stanford University Press.

Canto-Lugo, Ramiro F.
1991 La Danza de Moros y Cristianos en México. Ph.D. Dissertation, University of California at Davis.

Carrasco, Pedro
1961 The Civil-Religious Hierarchy in Mesoamerican Communities: Pre-Spanish Background and Colonial Development. *American Anthropologist* 63:484–497.

Cashion, Susan V.
1983 Dance Ritual and Cultural Values in a Mexican Village: Festival of Santo Santiago. Ph.D. dissertation. Stanford University.

Cheetham, Nicolas
1974 *New Spain: The Birth of Modern Mexico*. London: Victor Gollancz.

Chevalier, François
1963 *Land and Society in Colonial Mexico*. Berkeley and Los Angeles: University of California Press.

Clavigero, Francisco Javier
1833 *Historia Antigua de Mexico y de su Conquista*. Guadalajara, Jalisco.

Clifford, James
1988   *The Predicament of Culture: Twentieth-Century Ethnography, Literature, and Art.* Cambridge: Harvard University Press.

Clifford, James, and George Marcus, eds.
1986   *Writing Culture: The Poetics and Politics of Ethnography.* Berkeley: University of California Press.

Cockcroft, James D.
1983   *Mexico: Class Formation, Capital Accumulation and the State.* New York: Monthly Review Press.

Comaroff, Jean, and John L. Comaroff
1991   *Of Revelation and Revolution: Christianity, Colonialism and Consciousness in South Africa.* Chicago and London: The University of Chicago Press.

Cook, Scott
1973   Economic Anthropology: Problems in Theory, Method, and Analysis. In *Handbook of Social and Cultural Anthropology.* John J. Honigmann, ed. Pp. 795–860. Chicago: Rand McNally College Publishing Company.

1966   The Obsolete "Anti-Market" Mentality: A Critique of the Substantive Approach to Economic Anthropology. *American Anthropologist* 68(2):323–345.

Corella, M. Antonieta L. Rebiel
1985   What Mexican Youth Learn From Commercial Television. *Studies in Latin American Popular Culture* 4:188–199.

Cox, Harvey
1969   *The Feast of Fools.* Cambridge: Harvard University Press.

Crumrine, Lynne
1969   *Ceremonial Exchange as a Mechanism in Tribal Integration among the Mayos of Northwest Mexico.* Anthropological Papers of the University of Arizona, 14. Tucson: The University of Arizona Press.

Crumrine, Lynne, and N. Ross Crumrine
1977   Ritual Symbolism in Folk and Ritual Drama: The Mayo Indian San Cayetano Velación, Sonora, Mexico. *Journal of American Folklore* 90:8–18.

Crumrine, N. Ross
1970   Ritual Drama and Culture Change. *Comparative Studies in Society and History* 12:361–372.

1967   Capakoba, The Mayo Easter Ceremonial Impersonator: Explanations of
        Ritual Clowning. *Journal for the Scientific Study of Religion* 8:1–22.

Dávila Garibi, J. Ignacio
1957   *Apuntes Para la Historia de la Iglesia en Guadalajara.* Vol. I. Mexico, D.F.: Ed-
        itorial Cultura.

1927   *Breves Apuntes de los Chimalhuacanos.* Guadalajara, Jalisco.

Davis, Natalie Z.
1978   Women on Top: Symbolic Inversion and Political Disorder in Early Mod-
        ern Europe. In *The Reversible World.* Barbara Babcock, ed. Pp. 147–190.
        Ithaca: Cornell University Press.

Dennis, Phillip
1975   The Role of the Drunk in a Oaxacan Village. *American Anthropologist*
        77(4):856–863

DeWalt, Billie R.
1975   Changes in the Cargo Systems of Mesoamerica. *Anthropological Quarterly*
        48:87–105.

Diaz, May
1966   *Tonalá: Conservatism, Responsibility and Authority in a Mexican Town.*
        Berkeley: University of California Press.

Dolgin, Janet L., David S. Kemnitzer, and David M. Schneider, eds.
1977   Introduction. In *Symbolic Anthropology: A Reader in the Study of Symbols and
        Meanings.* Pp. 3–43. New York: Columbia University Press.

Dominguez, Jorge I., ed.
1982   *Mexico's Political Economy: Challenge at Home and Abroad.* Beverly Hills: Sage
        Publications.

Duvignaud, Jean
1976   Festivals: A Sociological Approach. *Cultures* 3(1):13–25.

Erasmus, Charles
1961   *Man Takes Control: Cultural Development and American Aide.* Minnesota:
        University of Minnesota Press.

Escuela de artes y oficios del estado
1912   *Indice Alfabético de los Lugares Habitados del Estado de Jalisco, 1910. . . .*
        Guadalajara: Tip. de la Escuela de artes y oficios del estado.

Estados Unidos Mexicanos. Dirección General de Estadística
1973   Noveno Censo General Población, 1970. 28 de enero. Localidades por entidad federativa y municipio con algunas características de su población y vivienda. Vol. 2, Hidalgo á Oaxaca. Mexico, D.F.: Estados Unidos Mexicanos. Dirección General de Estadística, p. 290.

1963   Octavo Censo de Población, 1960, Jalisco. Mexico, D.F.: Estados Unidos Mexicanos. Dirección General de Estadistica, p. 151.

1952   Séptimo Censo de Población, 1950, Jalisco. Mexico, D.F.: Estados Unidos Mexicanos. Dirección General de Estadistica, p. 328.

1943   Sexto Censo de Población, 1940, Jalisco. Mexico, D.F.: Estados Unidos Mexicanos. Dirección General de Estadistica, p. 246.

Etienne, Mona, and Eleanor Leacock, eds.
1980   *Women and Colonization: Anthropological Perspectives.* New York: Praeger Publishers.

Ferguson, James
1988   Cultural Exchange. New Developments in the Anthropology of Commodities. *Cultural Anthropology* 4(3):488–513.

Fletcher, Richard A.
1984   *Saint James Catapult: The Life and Times of Diego Gelmirez.* Oxford: Clarendon Press.

Foster, George
1948   The Current Status of Mexican Indian Folklore Studies. *Journal of American Folklore* 61:368–382.

Friedlander, Judith
1981   The Secularization of the Cargo System: An Example from Postrevolutionary Central Mexico. *Latin American Research Review* 16(2):132–143.

1975   *Being Indian in Hueyapan: A Study of Forced Identity in Contemporary Mexico.* New York: St. Martin's Press.

García Barajas, Eugenio
1986   Los Tastoanes, una viva tradición en Jocotán. In *Metropoli: Ocho Columnas* (Guadalajara, Mexico). September 10, p. 8B.

Garcia-Canclini, Nestor
1989   *Culturas hibridas: estrategias para entrar y salir de la modernidad.* Mexico, D.F.: Grijalbo: Consejo Nacional para la Cultura y las Artes.

Geertz, Clifford
1973   Deep Play: Notes on the Balinese Cockfight. In *Interpretations of Culture.* New York: Basic Books.

Gonzalez Navarro, Moises
1953   *Repartimiento de indios en Nueva Galicia.* Mexico.

Gerhard, Peter
1982   *The North Frontier of New Spain.* Princeton: Princeton University Press.

Gossen, Gary
1974   *Chamulas in the World of the Sun; Time and Space in a Maya Oral Tradition.* Cambridge: Harvard University Press.

1993   *South and Meso-American Native Spirituality: From the Cult of the Feathered Serpent to the Theology of Liberation.* New York: Crossroad.

Greenberg, James B.
1981   *Santiago's Sword: Chatino Peasant Religion and Economics.* Berkeley: University of California Press.

Guerrero Guerrero, Raul
1980   *El Pulque: Religion, Cultura, Folklore.* Mexico: SEP/INAH.

Hadley-Garcia, George
1990   *Hispanic Hollywood.* New York: Carol Publishing Group, 1990.

Hansen, Roger
1971   *The Politics of Mexican Development.* Baltimore: The Johns Hopkins Press.

Haring, C. H.
1974   *The Spanish Empire in America.* New York: Harcourt, Brace and World.

Hellman, Judith Adler
1983   *Mexico in Crisis.* New York: Holmes & Meier Publishers. Second edition.

Hieb, Louis A.
1972   Meaning and Mismeaning: Toward an Understanding of the Ritual Clown. In *New Perspectives on the Pueblos.* Alfonso Ortiz, ed. Pp. 163–196. Albuquerque: University of New Mexico Press.

Hill, Jonathan, ed.
1988   *Rethinking Myth and History: Indigenous South American Perspectives on the Past.* Urbana and Chicago: University of Illinois Press.

Huizinga, Johan
1955   *Homo Ludens: A Study of the Play Element in Culture.* Boston: Beacon Press.

Hunt, Eva
1977   *The Transformation of the Hummingbird.* Ithaca: Cornell University Press.

Hyde, Lewis
1983   *The Gift: Imagination and the Erotic Life of Poverty.* New York: Vintage Books.

Ingham, John M.
1986   *Mary, Michael, and Lucifer: Folk Catholicism in Central Mexico.* Austin: University of Texas Press.

Kendrick, T. D.
1960   *St. James in Spain.* London: Methuen.

Klor de Alva, Jorge
1993   Aztec Spirituality and Nahuatized Christianity. In *South and Meso-American Native Spirituality.* Gary Gossen, ed. Pp. 173–197. New York: The Crossroad Publishing Company.

1980   Spiritual Warfare in Mexico: Christianity and the Aztecs. Ph.D. dissertation. The University of California at Santa Cruz.

Kondo, Dorinne
1986   Dissolution and Reconstitution of Self: Implications for Anthropological Epistemology. *Cultural Anthropology* 1:74–88.

Kurath, Gertrude
1949a   Dance Folk and Primitive. In *The Standard Dictionary of Folklore, Mythology and Legend* 1:279–280. Maria Leach, ed. Vol I. Pp. 279–280. New York: Funk & Wagnalls.

1949b   Mexican Moriscas: A Problem in Dance Acculturation. *Journal of American Folklore* 62:87–106.

Lachmann, Renate
1988   Bakhtin and Carnival: Culture as Counter-Culture. *Cultural Critique* 11(Winter):115–152.

Lavenda, Robert H.
1986   Festivals and Carnivals. In *Handbook of Latin American Popular Culture.*
       Harold E. Hinds, Jr. and Charles M. Tatum, eds. Pp. 191–205. Westport,
       Connecticut: Greenwood Press.

Limón, Jose E.
1989   Representation, Ethnicity and the Precursory Ethnography. A contribution
       to the School of American Research Seminar "Representing Anthropol-
       ogy." School of American Research. Santa Fe, New Mexico.

1986   Mexican Speech Play: History and the Psychological Discourses of Power.
       Presented at a special invited session on Language and Political Economy
       at the American Anthropological Association Annual Meetings. Phila-
       delphia, Pennsylvania.

Lindley, Richard B.
1983   *Haciendas and Economic Development: Guadalajara, Mexico, at Independence.*
       Austin: University of Texas Press.

Logan, Kathleen
1984   *Haciendo Pueblo: The Development of a Guadalajaran Suburb.* Alabama: The
       University of Alabama Press.

Lomnitz, Larissa
1977   *Networks and Marginality: Life in a Mexican Shantytown.* New York: Aca-
       demia Press.

Lopez Portillo y Weber, José
1939   La Rebelión de la Nueva Galicia. *Instituto Panamericano de Geografía e Histo-
       ria* 37.

1935   *La Conquista de la Nueva Galicia.* Mexico: Talleres Gráficos de la Nación.

Makarius, Laura
1970   Ritual Clowns and Symbolic Behavior. *Diogenes* 69:44–73.

Marcus, George E.
1986   Afterword: Ethnographic Writing and Anthropological Careers. In *Writing
       Culture: The Poetics and Politics of Ethnography.* James Clifford and George E.
       Marcus, eds. Pp. 262–266. Berkeley: University of California Press.

Martin, Christopher J.
1994   *Schooling in Mexico: Staying In or Dropping Out.* Aldershot: Avebury.

Marzal, Manuel M.

1993   Transplanted Spanish Catholicism. In *South and Meso-American Native Spirituality.* Gary Gossen, ed. Pp. 140–172. New York: The Crossroad Publishing Company.

Mata Torres, Ramón

1987   *Los tastuanes de Nextipac.* Guadalajara, Jalisco, Mexico: Gobierno de Jalisco, Secretaría General, Unidad Editorial.

1986   La Fiesta de los Tastoanes. In *El Informador* (Guadalajara, Mexico). September 7. Suplemento Cultural, p. 16.

Mattelart, Armand

1985   The Nature of Communications Practice in a Dependent Society. *Latin American Perspectives* 5(1):13–34.

Matthews, Holly F.

1985   "We Are Mayordomo": A Reinterpretation of Women's Roles in the Mexican Cargo System. *American Ethnologist* 12:285–301.

Mauss, Marcel

1967   *The Gift: Forms and Functions of Exchange in Archaic Society.* Ian Cunnison, trans. London: Cohen & West. Originally published 1925.

McDowell, John H.

1983   Children's Folklore. In *Handbook of American Folklore.* Richard Dorson, ed. Pp. 314–322. Bloomington: Indiana University Press.

Mechling, Jay

1986   Children's Folklore. In *Folk Groups and Folklore Genres: An Introduction.* Elliot Oring, ed. Pp. 91–121. Logan, Utah: Utah State University Press.

Mesnil, Marianne

1976   The Masked Festival: Disguise or Affirmation. *Cultures* 3(2):11–29.

1987   Place and Time in the Carnivalesque Festival. In *Time Out of Time.* Alessandro Falassi, ed. Pp. 184–196. Albuquerque: University of New Mexico Press.

Meyer, Michael C., and William L. Sherman

1983   *The Course of Mexican History.* New York: Oxford University Press. Second edition.

Monaghan, John
1990   Reciprocity, Redistribution, and the Transaction of Value in the Meso-
        american Fiesta. *American Ethnologist* 17(4):758–774.

Mota y Escobar, Alonso de la
1966   *Descripción Geográfica de los Reinos de la Nueva Galicia, Nueva Vizcaya y
        Nuevo Leon.* Guadalajara, Mexico: Instituto Jalisciense de Antropología e
        Historia.

Mota Padilla, Matias Angel de la
1870   *Historia de la Conquista de la Nueva Galicia.* Mexico.

Nahmad, Salomon
1976   Mexican Feasts: Syncretism and Cultural Identity. *Cultures* 3(2):45–58.

Nájera, Olga
1983   La Fiesta de Los Tastoanes: A Traditional Festival in a Jalisco Town. Mas-
        ter's Thesis. The University of Texas at Austin.

Nájera-Ramírez, Olga
1988   Ideology and Social Process in La Fiesta de los Tastoanes. Ph.D. Disserta-
        tion. The University of Texas at Austin.

1988   The Representation of Gender in Fieldwork and Festival in Central Mex-
        ico. Paper presented at the American Anthropological Association Meet-
        ings on November 16, 1988, Phoenix, Arizona.

Nash, June
1980   Aztec Women: The Transition from Status to Class in Empire and Colony.
        In *Women and Colonization: Anthropological Perspectives.* Mona Etienne and
        Eleanor Leacock, eds. Pp. 134–148. New York: Praeger Publishers.

1968   The Passion Play in Maya Indian Communities. In *Comparative Studies in
        Society and History* 10:318–327.

Navarrete, Ignacio
1872   *Compendio de la Historia de Jalisco.* Guadalajara, Mexico.

Nayaran, Kirin
1993   How Native is a "Native" Anthropologist? *American Anthropologist* 95:671–
        686.

Needham, Rodney
1979   Percussion and Transition. In *Reader in Comparative Religion*. William A. Lessa and Evon Z. Vogt, eds. Pp. 311–317. New York: Harper and Row, Publishers, Inc.

Needler, Martin C.
1982   *Mexican Politics: The Containment of Conflict*. New York: Praeger Publishers.

Newell G., Roberto, and Luis Rubio F.
1984   *Mexico's Dilemma: The Political Origins of Economic Crisis*. Boulder: Westview Press.

Ong, Walter
1982   *Orality and Literacy: The Technologizing of the Word*. London and New York: Routledge.

Ortner, Sherry
1973   On Key Symbols. *American Anthropologist* 75:1338–1346.

Paredes, Américo
1977   Ethnographic Work Among Minorities: A Folklorist's Perspective. *New Scholar* 6:1–32.

Parry, J. H.
1948   *The Audiencia of New Galicia in the Sixteenth Century*. Cambridge: Cambridge University Press.

Peacock, James
1978   Symbolic Reversal and Social History: Transvestites and Clowns of Java. In *The Reversible World*. Barbara Babcock, ed. Pp. 209–224. Ithaca: Cornell University Press.

Peña, Guillermo de la
1981   *A Legacy of Promises: Agriculture, Politics, and Ritual in the Morelos Highlands of Mexico*. Austin: University of Texas Press.

Peña, Guillermo de la, and Agustin Escobar, eds.
1986   *Cambio regional, mercado de trabajo y vida obrera en Jalisco*. 1ª ed. Guadalajara, Jalisco, Mexico: Colegio de Jalisco.

Pettit, Arthur G.
1980   *Images of the Mexican American in Fiction and Film*. College Station: Texas A & M University Press.

Pike, Frederick
1990   Latin America. In *The Oxford Illustrated History of Christianity.* John
       McManners, ed. Pp. 420–455. New York: Oxford University Press.

Ramírez Flores, Ignacio
1980   *Lenguas Indigenas de Jalisco.* Guadalajara, Jalisco: Gobierno del Estado de
       Jalisco, Secretaría General de Gobierno, Unidad Editorial.

Ravicz, Marilyn Ekdahl
1970   *Early Colonial Religious Drama in Mexico: From Tzompantli to Golgotha.*
       Washington: Catholic University of America Press.

Ricard, Robert
1966   *The Spiritual Conquest of Mexico.* Berkeley: University of California Press.

Riviere D'Arc, Helene
1973   *Guadalajara y Su Region.* Mexico D.F.: Secretaría de Educación Pública/
       Setentas.

Rogers, Susan Carol
1975   Female Forms of Power and the Myth of Male Dominance: A Model of Fe-
       male/Male Interaction in Peasant Society. *American Ethnologist* 2:727–756.

Root, Deborah
1988   The Imperial Signifier: Todorov and the Conquest of Mexico. *Cultural Cri-
       tique* 9(Spring):197–219.

Rosaldo, Renato
1989   *Culture and Truth: The Remaking of Social Analysis.* Boston: Beacon Press.

1985   Chicano Studies, 1970–1984. *Annual Review of Anthropology* 14:405–427.

Roseberry, William
1989   *Anthropologies and Histories: Essays in Culture, History, and Political Economy.*
       New Brunswick: Rutgers University Press.

Roseberry, William, and Jay Obrien, eds.
1991   Introduction. In *Golden Ages, Dark Ages: Imagining the Past in Anthropology
       and History.* Berkeley: University of California Press.

Rowe, William, and Vivian Schelling
1991   *Memory and Modernity: Popular Culture in Latin America.* London and New
       York: Verso.

Rudé, George
1980   *Ideology and Popular Protest.* New York: Pantheon Books.

Rus, Jan, and Robert Wasserstrom
1980   Civil-Religious Hierarchies in Central Chiapas: A Critical Perspective. *American Ethnologist* 7(3):466–478.

Ryan, John Morris, et al.
1970   *Area Handbook for Mexico.* Washington D.C.: U.S. Government Printing Office.

Sahagún, Fray Bernardino de
1932   *Historia general de la cosas de Nueva España.* Volume 1. Translated by Fanny R. Bandelier. Nashville, Tennessee: Fisk University Press.

Sanches Flores, Francisco
1976   *Danzas Fundamentales de Jalisco.* Mexico: FONADAN.

Sanday, Peggy Reeves
1981   *Female Power and Male Dominance: On the Origins of Sexual Inequality.* Cambridge: Cambridge University Press.

Sandstrom, Alan R.
1982   The Tonantsi Cult of Eastern Nahua. In *Mother Worship: Theme and Variations.* James Preston, ed. Pp. 23–50. Chapel Hill: University of North Carolina Press.

Santoscoy, D. Alberto
1889   *Apuntamentos Históricos y Biográficos Jaliscienses: Los Primeros Conquistadores en el Territorio; El Primer Martir Franciscano; Los Tastuanes.* Guadalajara, Jalisco.

Scott, James
1976   *The Moral Economy of the Peasant: Rebellion and Subsistence in Southeast Asia.* New Haven: Yale University Press.

1977   Hegemony and the Peasantry. *Politics and Society* 7(3):267–296.

Secretaría de Fomento
1905   *Censo General de la República Mexicana, Estado de Jalisco.* Mexico: Secretaría de Fomento.

Silverblatt, Irene

1988   Political Memories and Colonizing Symbols: Santiago and the Mountain
        Gods of Colonial Peru. In *Rethinking Myth and History: Indigenous South
        American Perspectives on the Past.* Jonathan D. Hill, ed. Pp. 174–195. Urbana
        and Chicago: University of Illinois.

1980   "The Universe has turned inside out . . . There is no justice for us here."
        Andean Women Under Spanish Rule. In *Women and Colonization: Anthropo-
        logical Perspectives.* Mona Etienne and Eleanor Leacock, eds. Pp. 149–185.
        New York: Praeger Publishers.

Simpson, Lesley Byrd

1966   *The Encomienda in New Spain.* Berkeley and Los Angeles: University of Cal-
        ifornia Press.

Smith, Robert J.

1975   *The Art of Festival.* Lawrence: University of Kansas. Publications in Anthro-
        pology, No. 6.

1972   Licentious Behavior in Hispanic Festivals. *Western Folklore* 31(4):290–298.

Smith, Walderman

1977   *The Fiesta System and Economic Change.* New York: Columbia University
        Press.

Sociedad Mexicana de Geografia y Estadistica

1941–   *Boletín de la Junta Auxiliar Jalisciense de la Sociedad Mexicana de Geografía y*
1942   *Estadística* 7(3):175–190.

Starkie, Walter Fitzwilliam

1965   *The Road to Santiago: Pilgrims of St. James.* Berkeley: University of California.

Starr, Frederick

1902   The Tastoanes. *Journal of American Folklore* 15(57):73–83.

Stephen, Lynn, and James Dow

1990   Introduction: Popular Religion in Mexico and Central America. In *Class,
        Politics and Popular Religion in Mexico and Central America.* Lynn Stephen
        and James Dow, eds. Pp. 1–24. Washington, D.C.: Society for Latin Amer-
        ican Anthropology: American Anthropological Association.

Stevenson, Robert M.

1952   *Music in Aztec and Inca Territory.* Berkeley: University of California Press.

Stoeltje, Beverly J.
1989   Festival. In *The International Encyclopedia of Communication*. Erik Barnouw,
       ed. New York and Oxford: Oxford University Press.

1987   Riding, Roping, and Reunion: Cowboy Festival. In *Time Out of Time*. Ales-
       sandro Falassi, ed. Pp. 137–151. Albuquerque: University of New Mexico.

1983   Festival in America. In *Handbook of American Folklore*. Richard M. Dorson,
       ed. Pp. 239–246. Bloomington: Indiana University Press.

1981   Cowboys and Clowns: Rodeo Specialists and the Ideology of Work and
       Play. In *"And Other Neighborly Names": Social Process and Cultural Image in
       Texas Folklore*. Richard Bauman and Roger Abrahams, eds. Pp. 123–151.
       Austin: University of Texas Press.

Stone, J. S.
1927   *The Cult of Santiago*. New York: Longmans, Green and Company.

Straubhaar, Joseph
1986   Television. In *Handbook of Latin American Popular Culture*. Harold E.
       Hinds, Jr. and Charles M. Tatum, eds. Pp. 111–134. Westport, Connecti-
       cut: Greenwood Press.

Tax, Sol
1953   *Penny Capitalism: A Guatemalan Indian Economy*. Washington, D.C.:
       Smithsonian Institute of Social Anthropology 16.

Tello, Fray Antonio
1891   *Libro Segundo de la Crónica Miscelanea en que se trata de la Conquista Espiritual
       y Temporal de la Santa Provincia de Xalisco*. Guadalajara, Jalisco.

Theriot, Nancy
1990   The Politics of 'Meaning Making': Feminist Hermeneutics, Language and
       Culture. In *Sexual Politics and Popular Culture*. Diane Raymond, ed. Bowling
       Green: Popular Press.

Thomas, Nicolas
1989   *Out of Time: History and Evolution in Anthropological Discourse*. Cambridge:
       Cambridge University Press.

Topete Bordes, Luis
1944   *Jalisco Precortesano*. Mexico, D.F.

Todorov, Tzvetan
1984   *The Conquest of America: The Question of the Other.* New York: Harper and
        Row.

Trexler, Richard C.
1982   From the Mouths of Babes: Christianization by Children in 16th Century
        New Spain. In *Religious Organization and Religious Experience.* J. Davis, ed.
        Pp. 115–136. London: Academic Press Inc.

Turner, Kay
1980   The Virgin of Sorrows Procession: A Brooklyn Inversion. In *Folklore Papers
        of the University Folklore Association.* No. 9. Austin: The Center for Intercul-
        tural Studies in Folklore and Ethnomusicology at the University of Texas.

Turner, Victor
1982   *From Ritual to Theatre: The Human Seriousness of Play.* New York City: Per-
        forming Arts Journal Publications.

Valle, Rafael Heliodoro
1949   *Santiago en America.* México, D.F.: Editorial Santiago.

Van Young, Eric
1984   Conflict and Solidarity in Indian Village Life: The Guadalajara Region in
        the Late Colonial Period. *Hispanic American Historical Review* 64(1):55–79.

1981   *Hacienda and Market in Eighteenth Century Mexico: The Rural Economy of the
        Guadalajara Region: 1675–1820.* Berkeley: University of California Press.

Vaughan, Mary K.
1982   *The State, Education, and Social Class in Mexico, 1880–1928.* DeKalb: North-
        ern Illinois University Press.

Vogt, Evon Z.
1965   Ceremonial Organization in Zinacantan. *Ethnology* 4: 39–52.

1955   A Study of the Southwestern Fiesta System as Exemplified by the Laguna
        Fiesta. *American Anthropologist* 57:820–839.

Warman, Arturo
1972   *Los Moros y Cristianos.* Mexico, D.F.: Secretaría de Educación Pública.

Weigle, Marta
1982   *Spiders and Spinsters: Women and Mythology.* Albuquerque: University of
        New Mexico Press.

White, Allon, and Peter Stallybrass
1986   *The Politics and Poetics of Transgression.* Ithaca, New York: Cornell University Press.

1988   The Struggle Over Bakhtin: Fraternal Reply to Robert Young. *Cultural Critique* 8(Spring):217–241.

Willeford, William
1969   *The Fool and his Scepter.* Evanston: Northwestern University Press.

Williams, Raymond
1982   *The Sociology of Culture.* New York: Schocken Books.

1977   *Marxism and Literature.* Oxford, England: Oxford University Press.

Wolf, Eric
1964   *Sons of the Shaking Earth.* Chicago: University of Chicago Press.

1957   Closed Corporate Communities in Mesoamerica and Central Java. *Southwestern Journal of Anthropology* 13:1–18.

Woll, Allen
1980   *The Latin Image in American Film.* Los Angeles: Latin American Center Publications.

Zavella, Patricia
1993   Feminist Insider Dilemmas — Constructing Ethnic Identity with Chicana Informants. *Frontiers* 13(3):53–76.

Index